ACHIEVING QTS

CROSS-CURRICULAR STRAND
TEACHING LITERACY ACROSS THE PRIMARY CURRICULUM

ACHIEVING QTS

CROSS–CURRICULAR STRAND

Teaching Literacy Across
the Primary Curriculum

David Wray

LearningMatters

First published in 2006 by Learning Matters Ltd.

British Library Cataloguing in Publication Data
A CIP record for this book is available from the British Library.

ISBN-13: 978 1 84445 008 4
ISBN-10: 1 84445 008 2

Cover and text design by Topics – The Creative Partnership
Project management by Deer Park Productions, Tavistock, Devon
Typeset by Pantek Arts Ltd, Maidstone, Kent
Printed and bound in Great Britain by Cromwell Press, Trowbridge, Wiltshire

Learning Matters Ltd

33 Southernhay East
Exeter EX1 1NX
Tel: 01392 215560
info@learningmatters.co.uk
www.learningmatters.co.uk

CONTENTS

QTS standards

This book is designed to help you meet the following standards for the award of QTS.

Those recommended for the award of QTS (Q) should:

1.5 Q
(a) Recognise the contribution that they and colleagues can make to the attainment, development and well-being of children and young people.

1.8 Q Adopt a creative and constructively critical approach towards innovation, adapting their practice where benefits and improvements are identified.

2.2 Q Know how to make effective provision for all those they teach, including those for whom English is an additional language, and how to take practical account of diversity and promote equality and inclusion in their teaching.

2.4 Q Have a secure knowledge and understanding of their subjects/curriculum areas to enable them to teach effectively across the age and ability range for which they are trained to teach.

2.9 Q Have a knowledge and understanding of a range of teaching, learning and behaviour management strategies and know how to use and adapt them to learners' needs.

3.5 Q
(a) Plan and teach lessons and sequences of lessons that are safe and well-organised, demonstrating secure subject knowledge relevant to the curricula across the age range for which they are trained.
(b) Use a range of teaching strategies and resources, including e-learning, taking practical account of diversity and promoting equality and inclusion.
(c) Provide opportunities for learners to develop their literacy, numeracy and ICT skills.

Objectives:

The aim of this section is to introduce you to:
1. *The cross-curricular nature of reading and writing.*
2. *The need to broaden the teaching of literacy beyond the literacy hour.*

Reading and writing in schools

'Reading' and 'writing' are both verbs which can be either transitive or intransitive. That is to say, they can either take a direct object or not. It makes perfectly good sense to say that a major aim of schooling is to produce children who can read and write, and here we are using these verbs intransitively. They are generic. Reading and writing are vital skills no matter what it is that you read or write.

But we can also include in our expectations the aim that our children will learn to read and to write *something*. This something (we might, for the want of a better word, call it 'text') includes a huge range of material, the sheer scope of which can often surprise even experienced teachers. As an example of this, I recently shadowed one primary child (a 9-year-old boy – a Year 4 in the English system) throughout most of a school day, making a note of anything he read or wrote (or at least was supposed to be reading or writing). Here is an edited list of what I witnessed.

Time	Location	Reading engaged in	Writing engaged in
8.55	Playground	Read a page from a comic with his friend	
9.05	Classroom	Read instructions on class whiteboard	Copied instruction into his workbook
9.15	Hall	Read hymn from overhead projector (OHP)	
9.30	Classroom	Read text on interactive whiteboard (IWB) Read list of 'strong' verbs on IWB Read aloud from his sentences to class	Wrote alternative verb into IWB text Wrote sentences using strong verbs Revised one sentence by changing verb spelling used
11.00	Classroom	Read maths problem on IWB Read teacher's answer ... *repeated several times* ... Read maths problem from workbook ... *repeated several times* ...	Wrote his answer on his mini whiteboard Ticked his answer ... *repeated several times* ... Wrote answers to maths problem ... *repeated several times* ...

Time	Location	Reading engaged in	Writing engaged in
12.10	Hall	Read lunch menu Read more from his comic Read a joke aloud to a friend	
1.10	Classroom	Read from his personal library book	Recorded pages read in his reading record book
1.20	Classroom	Read science investigation instructions from whiteboard Reread instructions from his book as he carried out the investigation … *repeated several times* …	Wrote instructions in his science book Wrote results of the investigation in his book … *repeated several times* …
2.20	Classroom	Read teacher's account of the investigation on whiteboard Read aloud some of his results for teacher to write	Wrote a summary of two sentences in his book about the investigation
2.35	Classroom	Read musical notations from whiteboard and played his castanets at appropriate points Read notation as the group played their composition back to class	Wrote notation for his group's musical composition
3.15	Classroom	Read class notice about a school trip which he had to take home to parents	Wrote notes about homework into his exercise book

What is perhaps a little surprising about this list is the revelation that just about every school event involved some kind of reading and writing. Some of this reading and writing was a focus of teaching, but, in most cases, the teacher just assumed this boy could do it. Her pedagogic attention was on other things for most of the school day.

Practical task

Literacy shadowing

Try to carry out a similar 'pupil shadowing' exercise with two children (more if you can manage it) that you come across in the course of teaching placements. All you will need is a simple notebook in which to record any examples of reading and writing you see during a day.

Make a note of what is being read or written, whether this involves individual or collaborative activity, and any outcome it has. Also note, in the case of classroom assigned reading and writing, whether the aim of the activity was to improve the child's literacy or whether it had different aims.

Look over what you have recorded and think about:

* *the range of reading and writing done;*

* *any particular difficulties experienced by the child;*

* *any assistance in reading and writing given by the teacher.*

Having done this kind of shadowing exercise with many primary children, what always surprises me is the sheer range of kinds of reading and writing that gets done. Even in the single example above, we see the reading of comics, instructions, hymns, individual words, maths text, menus, jokes, science instructions, science data, reports, musical notation, notices, and a similarly wide range of writing experiences. When we use reading and writing transitively, it is clear that they take a lot of direct objects.

Also, it is quite likely that for most of the reading and writing a child does in a school day, because the reading and writing itself are not the main focus of the task, the child gets little support in the use of these skills. He/she is expected to 'just do it', and support and discussion are focused on the outcomes, that is, the subject content.

The National Literacy Strategy approach

When the National Literacy Strategy (Department for Education and Employment (DfEE), 1998) was first introduced into primary schools in England, its main focus was upon the explicit, dedicated teaching of literacy, within tightly-defined and earmarked class time – reading and writing viewed intransitively. Such explicit attention was probably necessary as there was evidence, especially at Key Stage 2, that many teachers were 'double-counting' teaching time, claiming to be giving children instruction and practice in reading and writing within the teaching of other subjects, such as history, environmental studies, etc.. The evidence suggested that such an approach risked literacy teaching being planned as an afterthought to the teaching of the subject content, and the assumption being made that the skills involved in reading and writing in these subject areas would simply be picked up by children through practice. Such an *ad hoc* approach is not likely, if applied widely, to lead to effective literacy learning.

Research insight

What do effective teachers do?

Our research (Wray et al., 2002), carried out in 1997, prior to the introduction of the National Literacy Strategy (NLS), discovered that effective literacy teachers were, in almost all cases, teaching literacy skills in a very explicit way. In fact, they were teaching versions of a literacy hour, at that time just an idea in the mind of the planners of the NLS.

Explicit and focused teaching of literacy is now, of course, thoroughly established in primary schools. More recently, schools and teachers have begun to interpret the literacy hour in a rather more flexible way, but nevertheless literacy teaching objectives are still at the forefront of their planning for the learning of their children. Such explicit and focused teaching, however, has brought with it its own problems, centred on the fact that there is also a curriculum outside of the literacy hour, and learning within this curriculum also requires the skilful use of literacy. The teaching of literacy across the curriculum has not disappeared from British primary schools, but it does receive a good deal less attention than it needs.

Aims for literacy across the curriculum

Teaching literacy across the curriculum has three major aims.

1. It should broaden and enhance children's command of literacy skills by giving them a range of different contexts in which to use and practise these skills. Literate people do not merely possess literacy skills – they know when and how to use them to solve problems involving text.

2. It should locate the teaching of the literacy skills central to a particular subject within that subject. The learning of a subject includes the learning of appropriate ways to communicate within that subject and the ways in which debate and development within the subject take place – often called the 'discourse' of the subject.

3. It should enhance the learning of the subject and children's motivations towards that learning. Learning the literacy of a subject is the key to successful learning in that subject.

Teachers in training, whatever their subject and age specialism, need to understand the importance of literacy in their teaching. The aim of this book is to explore in some detail approaches to teaching and developing literacy in a range of subject areas.

Summary

- **When you are reading and writing, you are reading and writing something.**
- **This something may include material from all curriculum areas.**
- **Thus literacy is inevitably a cross-curricular process.**
- **For literacy to be used effectively as a tool for learning, it needs to be taught not just in discrete lessons, but in many and varied contexts.**

References and further reading

DfEE (1998) *The National Literacy Strategy: Framework for Teaching* London: Department for Education and Employment (now the Department for Education and Skills (DfES).

Wray, D., Medwell, J., Fox, R. and Poulson, L. (2002) *Teaching literacy effectively*. London: Routledge Falmer. This book reports a detailed study of teachers known to be effective teachers of literacy. A number of common characteristics of such teachers are described, including their use of meaning-focused approaches to reading and writing, and their explicit teaching of literacy skills within meaningful contexts.

1 WHY LITERACY ACROSS THE PRIMARY CURRICULUM?

Chapter objectives:

The aim of this chapter is to introduce you to:
- *the nature of literacy as a set of specific or generic skills;*
- *the ways in which teaching literacy in a range of curriculum subjects may enhance achievement in those subjects as well as in literacy.*

Introduction

Discussions about the teaching of literacy across the curriculum often meet the objection from specialists in curriculum subjects other than English that this approach risks the 'sacrifice' of their subjects to the needs of English and literacy. The case needs to be made that enhanced attention to literacy swithin other curriculum subjects is not simply a case of literacy 'stealing' more time for itself – it could also lead to enhanced learning and teaching effectiveness within those subjects themselves. It is the purpose of this chapter to advance such a case, and to develop a rationale for the teaching of literacy across the curriculum.

Literacy: generic or specific skills?

The belief that reading and writing are generic skills predominated for many years among teachers and is probably still predominant among lay people. It is sometimes seen in media representations of literacy teaching and in some published teaching materials.

- **If only our children were taught to spell, they would be able to write with complete confidence.**
- **There are forty-four sounds in English. If children learn all of these sounds, they will be able to read anything.**

A generic skill is one that, once learned, can be applied in any situation. For example, if I learn the generic skill of hammering a nail, it follows that I can then hammer any nail. If I learn how to ride a bicycle, I can then ride any bicycle. The same reasoning applied to literacy produces the claim that: once I learn how to read, then I can read anything; once I learn how to write, then I can write anything. This view assumes that if children can read or write words, they can read or write sentences; if they can read or write sentences, they can read or write stories; and, if they can read or write stories, they then have what it takes to read or write history texts, science texts, and so on.

We now know, however, that reading and writing are not generic skills. Even adults who are able to read novels, poetry and information books proficiently can have trouble with insurance policies, tax forms, directions for putting together DIY furniture, computer manuals, and information material on topics unfamiliar to them. Similarly, adults who can write perfectly good accounts of their careers can fail completely to rework the information in these accounts into a persuasive argument as to why they are the best people for particular jobs.

In fact, there are no truly generic skills. Just because I can ride an ordinary bicycle does not mean that I can ride a multi-speed racing bike. Similarly, different nails are used in different materials for different purposes, and they are not all hammered the same way. We learn things not in isolation, but in a context. We learn how to hammer a particular kind of nail into a particular material using a particular hammer. If the situation changes – if the nails, material or hammer are different – then what I have already learned may actually be a hindrance. Think about someone who has learned to hit a large, long nail very hard to drive it deeply into a wooden beam. Now he has a short, thin nail that he wants to drive into a plaster wall to hang a picture. If he applies his learnt nail-driving skill in this situation, he may crack the plaster, bend the nail, hit his thumb, or, even if all else goes well, drive the nail too far into the wall. Hammering short, thin nails demands a different technique, and different skills, to hammering large, long nails.

Nothing we learn can be transferred directly to all situations. However, we do use what we already know to deal with new situations. When we must hammer a new kind of nail, we use what we already know from past experiences with nails, plaster and picture-hanging and put it all together to hypothesise what to do. We draw on all our relevant past experiences to deal with new situations. If the new experience is very similar to our past experiences, our behaviour may be very similar to past behaviour. But if the new experience is dissimilar, our previous experiences may not be very helpful.

What does this mean for literacy? Like everything else, reading and writing are learnt in particular contexts. We learn how to read and write particular texts and we develop a number of strategies for achieving our goals.

When the context changes – when we are faced with different reading or writing tasks, with different purposes – we try to use what we have learnt from previous literacy experiences. However, what we learnt during these experiences may not work in the new situation. Strategies developed for hitting one kind of nail do not work with all nails, and strategies learned for reading or writing one kind of text do not necessarily work with all texts.

Literacy skills are always used within a context and are specific to that context. Four main factors influence the use of these skills – the reader or writer, the kind of text being read or written, the topic or content of that text and the situation within which the reading or writing takes place. These factors overlap and interact to affect the nature of the literacy employed at any given time.

The reader/writer

The state of the reader or writer affects the process of reading or writing. Physical and emotional states such as tiredness, hunger and mood can all make a difference to the way readers approach texts and writers set about composing. A child, for example, whose parents are divorcing, might be upset and unable to concentrate on reading a science text. On the other hand, the same child may eagerly read a story about a child of divorced parents or information material about coping with divorce.

The prior knowledge of readers/writers is also important. A reader's familiarity both with the topics and the formats of text substantially influences his/her ability to understand these texts. If the topic is very familiar, then a reader may have some difficulty but will probably be able to work through any problems. A child who knows about space exploration can often read new material about space missions even if the format and the vocabulary are not completely familiar. If both topic and format are unfamiliar, however, then readers are likely to have difficulty comprehending. This is why so many adults have trouble with, for example, income tax forms. We know little about the topic — we are not familiar with the rules and regulations regarding taxes. In addition, we rarely read material that is structured like the tax form and the directions for completing it. Because both the topic and the format are unfamiliar, we have trouble with this reading. Tax accountants, on the other hand, know the rules and regulations governing income taxes and, having read thousands of these forms and directions, are very familiar with their structure. Their familiarity with both the topic and format makes income tax forms very readable for them.

Practical task

The effect of readers' and writers' experiences

Collect a few examples for your classroom experience where a child has seemed able to read or write something in one context but not in another. Some examples you might have seen include those below.

- *A child who spells words correctly in a spelling text but wrongly when he/she uses these words in an extended piece of writing.*

- *A child who can read 'difficult' words in an information book (think 'velociraptor' and 'gigantosaurus') but stumbles over apparently simpler words in a different text.*

How might you explain these variations in performance? What implications do they have for you as a teacher of literacy?

The text

The vocabulary, sentence structure and organisational patterns of texts vary. While fictional pieces differ from poems and information texts, there are also differences within each type. All poems are not alike, and it demands different textual knowledge to read or write a haiku or a ballad. Similarly, not all information texts are the same. The difference between, say, a history text and a science text can be as great as between a history text and a story. Because each type of text needs to be read differently, these variations affect the reading process. Composing these text types will also affect the writing process.

Texts, especially information texts, also contain a wide variety of content material. There will be marked vocabulary and grammatical differences between texts because of this content difference. Of these differences, vocabulary is the most widely recognised. Most people will know, for example, that a text containing words such as 'perimeter', 'angle', 'equation' and 'hypotenuse' will usually have mathematical content, even though they might not be sufficiently familiar with the vocabulary to understand (or write) such a text effectively. Grammar, however, is also content specific. To take one example, the sentence, 'Harry carefully added the sparkling white powder to the rest of the ingredients' could probably only occur in a work of fiction. The subject of the sentence is a named person, the sentence is active and declarative, and its object is given two adjectives, one of which suggests a subjective judgement. A similar sentence about science content would probably have read, 'The white powder was added to the mixture'. Note the use of the passive, the lack of subjective description and the vanishing subject.

If they are to understand the texts they read, and if they are to write text successfully, readers/writers need to have some familiarity with the vocabulary and grammar of texts in different content areas.

Context

The context of the reading/writing situation includes the physical location of the reader/writer, the constraints and expectations surrounding the reading/writing, and its purpose. For example, the same material found in a textbook, a newspaper, an advertisement, or a novel will not be read in the same way. Readers tend to have different expectations of various types of material and these expectations influence the process of their reading. They might expect newspapers to be easy to read as well as biased, or novels to focus on human events in chronological order and to be enjoyable, or textbooks to contain lists of facts, have a categorical, logical organisation, and to be boring and hard to read. Because of these expectations, they approach these reading materials differently.

Similarly, if a writer's purpose is to produce a story in an examination, he or she will tackle this task very differently than if the purpose were to add an entry to a personal diary. Writing style, the balance of attention between composing ideas and transcribing them and the use of redrafting may all differ widely between these two acts of writing.

Practical task

Children's views about text differences

One of the best ways to appreciate the effects of textual differences is to ask children how they see the situation. Choose a group of three or four talkative children and ask them firstly what kinds of material they prefer to read. They will undoubtedly have preferences. Then ask them why they like or dislike particular types of reading materials. Their answers may focus on content – for example, they like information books because they contain interesting facts. Try to get them to comment also on the ways different texts are laid out and the effects that may have on their enjoyment, and on the circumstances in which they might read, or be required to read, certain texts and, again, effects of these circumstances on their enjoyment.

Literacy variation

This variation between different experiences of reading and writing has important consequences for the teaching of literacy in schools. The first important piece of information all teachers need to know is that readers do not read different sorts of texts in the same way. A reader who is proficient in some contexts may lack proficiency in others. At primary level, we typically make judgements about children's reading abilities on the basis of their performance in reading fiction texts, yet the types of text read and the purposes for reading them change the nature of the interaction between the reader and text. We do not read fiction in the same way that we read non-fiction, and even the way we read fiction will depend on factors well beyond the text itself (Traves, 1994). Reading *Jane Eyre* on the beach for relaxation is quite different from reading it for a GCSE examination or as part of a PhD on the construction of women in nineteenth-century literature. The words on the page remain the same but the experience and meaning of the reading vary significantly. According to Lunzer and Gardner (1984), it is quite common for children to take it for granted that to read correctly is to understand, as if recognising the words and what they mean was all there was to it. This assumption may be true in some cases – reading an exciting story may well proceed in this fashion. But most reading for information and subject-based reading is done quite differently. Much of it requires the reader to skim and scan for potentially useful passages, to make repeated readings and rereadings of passages to establish and check for meaning, and to pause to reflect on and summarise developing ideas. The evidence suggests that many children are less competent at this sort of reading than in the reading of fiction (Wray and Lewis, 1997).

A parallel picture applies to writing. Wray and Lewis (1997) outline a range of evidence that the writing experience of primary children is, firstly, predominantly fiction-based, and, secondly, that non-fiction writing tends to consist of the production of narrative recounts (in the next chapter we will explore in more detail the differences between texts such as recounts and other texts). Yet writing in different curriculum subjects will, typically, demand different processes, structures and language choices. Even when different subjects demand what seem at first sight to be similar text types, the differences will still be considerable. For example, children may be asked to explain phenomena in science and in history, but the precise ways in which they write these explanations will be different. Each subject has a distinct 'discourse style' over and above the textual range which characterises work in that subject.

Research insight

Writing in different disciplines

In his book **Disciplinary discourses** *(Hyland, 2000), Ken Hyland explores in detail the ways in which writers in different academic disciplines (e.g. physics, engineering, sociology, philosophy, linguistics) write differently. The question he asks is, basically, 'Why do engineers "report" while philosophers "argue" and biologists "describe"?' And how do these written forms differ? His argument is that writing in different disciplines obeys fundamentally different rules. Disciplines, from biology to marketing, are produced and continually reproduced by the writing that characterises them, and different disciplinary practices and values are revealed in scholars' use of particular genre conventions. Even within a discipline, different written forms are constructed differently. There is a distinction, for example, between the scientific letter and the traditional peer-reviewed article, the scientific letter being a fast way of getting news to the scientific community. In the scientific letter, boldness and tentativeness co-exist. The author's claims must be sufficiently compelling to hold the reader's attention, yet not so brash as to constitute a breach of scientific reporting conventions. Hyland analyses the role played in this by 'hedges' and 'boosters'. He finds, for example, that scientific letters make much greater use of boosters (e.g. evidently, clearly, obviously) than do traditional research articles, but that hedges (e.g. may, seem, possibly) are used even more frequently than boosters.*

Learning to handle the complexities of the writing choices faced within a discipline is, Hyland argues, a crucial element in achieving success within that discipline.

All of this suggests, then, that the teaching of generic literacy skills will only take children so far as they begin to develop subject-based expertise. Specific reading and writing skills are necessary to effective learning and performance in history, and these are different from the specific skills necessary in science, etc.. The deliberate teaching of these specific skills within the context of the subject area to which they belong will enhance children's command of literacy. But it will also – and this, for subject specialists, is a crucial argument – enhance children's learning and achievements within those subjects. It is towards evidence in support of this contention that we now turn.

Literacy enhances subject learning

A number of research studies (although the vast majority of them are US-based) have explored the effects on children's subject learning of embedding with subject teaching a specific attention to literacy skills. In the US, much of this work has been conducted under the heading of 'integrated instruction', defined by Goodlad and Su (1992, p. 330) as 'intended to bring into close relationship such elements as concepts, skills, and values so that they are mutually reinforcing'. The breaking down of curriculum boundaries implied by this aim has been comparatively rare and subject-focused curricula have tended to work against it. Studies into the effects of interdisciplinary links have, therefore, tended to preserve disciplinary boundaries and research has focused on such linkings as science and literacy, mathematics and literacy, and humanities and literacy.

Science and literacy

Interdisciplinary approaches involving science have usually involved the use of literature and authentic resource materials, and made a conscious effort to teach specific literacy skills and strategies within the context of learning science (e.g. Palincsar and Herrenkohl, 1999; Bristor, 1994; Morrow et al., 1997).

Bristor (1994) described the results of a study of science and literacy integration. These researchers designed a programme in which they drew on research in literacy to build children's background knowledge before they were asked to read science texts. They also used literature with science themes and involved children in dramatic play related to these themes. Gains were found in children's achievement in both reading and in science and these were greater than those made by control groups who were taught science and literacy separately. The children following the integrated teaching also developed more positive attitudes towards science and a greater self-confidence about their own abilities.

Morrow et al. (1997) made similar findings. Children were taught literacy (in this case through the use of children's literature) and science together. They were tested before and after a year-long intervention, using informal and standardised tests to evaluate their growth in literacy skills and science knowledge. On almost all measures children following the integrated teaching approach did better than control groups.

Moore and Moore (1989) summarise research into the effects of integrating science learning with the learning of strategies for reading text more effectively, and conclude that when science and literacy are integrated, children enhance their learning of both science and literacy skills.

Mathematics and literacy

Winograd and Higgins (1995) describe their approach to integrating literacy teaching into the mathematics curriculum through child-devised story problems. They detail the integration of mathematical reasoning, small-group discussions, and writing activities. They show how the need to create daily story problems led children to observe events outside the classroom as sources of such problems (e.g. one child interviewed his father about his job sanding streets after a snowfall). Winograd and Higgins suggest that such curriculum integration helped these children move beyond the surface features of a story problem to a deeper consideration of its meaning, and thus enhanced their abilities to solve problems. Thus, mathematical problem-solving skills and the skills of writing meaningful text were both enhanced.

Humanities and literacy

A number of studies have examined connections between humanities work and literacy. The greater popularity of such work is not, perhaps, surprising when one considers that, for subjects such as history, social and moral education, the raw material of learning tends to be texts of one form of another. Studies suggest that the integration of literary material into humanities work can improve children's motivation to learn and the extent of this content learning.

For example, Levstick's (1990) research with children aged from 6 to 12 years suggested that literature could be motivating to history learning. Children across these age levels were very interested in the lives of human beings, and literature provided them with a way of studying these and making active connections to their own experiences.

Other research (e.g. Smith 1993; Smith et al., 1992) has found that children remembered more and had better conceptual understanding when literacy and humanities were integrated. Smith tested the changes in children's memories of historical events after using a variety of historical fiction to supplement their history teaching. His results indicated that these children remembered up to 60 per cent more information about historical events than did children who were not introduced to the historical fiction. Guzzetti et al.'s (1992) comparison of 11-year-olds' learning about China through textbooks or a mixture of textbooks and literature produced similar findings.

In the UK, Cottingham and Daborn (2000) have reported on their deliberate integration of literacy work into their teaching of history. Although focused on secondary classrooms, this study has a number of implications for primary practice. In the study, a variety of techniques were used to engage the children with the text, including directed activities related to texts (DARTS) such as cloze or highlighting individual words which related to historical causes. The final pupil outcome was an extended piece of writing, guided by a writing frame (many of the teaching ideas used in this study were derived from Wray and Lewis, 1997). Analysis of the children's written work and interviews with them suggested that children who had studied their history through such literacy-focused methods were more successful in that history than children in a control group. They were given a model for ways of gaining meaning from text and were substantially more successful in their final written tasks.

Finally, Guthrie et al. (1994) report their research into the use of what they refer to as 'concept-oriented reading instruction' – a teaching approach involving the deliberate integration of a number of curriculum subjects, and for which the best known British parallel is 'project work'. They found significant benefits to children from this approach in terms of their motivation to engage in active reading and their use of literacy skills such as the ability to search and retrieve information, to comprehend what they read and to compose reports about content topics to be read by peers.

Summary

This chapter has tried to make a case for the teaching of literacy across the curriculum, in addition to its teaching in separate, focused lessons. I have put forward, and illustrated, two main arguments.

1. Literacy is not a generic skill but its precise operation varies according to the context in which it is used, the task to which it is applied and the connections made by a reader/writer to that context and task. One easy way of appreciating the problems caused by seeing literacy as generic is to imagine that your course tutors have announced they will be assessing your ability to read and write and that they have decided to do this through your performance on a mathematics examination. You do read and write in mathematics, don't you? So why does the context of a mathematics examination seem an unfair way of assessing your reading and writing? Your probable answer, that you don't read and write as well in mathematics as you do in subjects, is precisely the point I am making here.

2. When we teach literacy in the context of other subject areas, we not only develop the literacy skills of learners, we also develop their understanding of, and achievements in, those subject areas. This kind of 'win–win' situation is actually quite unusual in education, so we would be remiss as teachers if we ignored its possibilities.

References and further reading

Bristor, V (1994) Combining reading and writing with science to enhance content area achievement and attitudes, *Reading Horizons*, 35 (1), pp. 31–43.

Cottingham, M and Daborn, J (2000) *What impact can developments in literacy teaching have on teaching and learning in history?* Teacher Training Agency Research Summary 133/8-00. London: Teacher Training Agency (TTA).

Goodlad, J and Su, Z (1992) The organisation of the curriculum, in Jackson, P. (ed.) *Handbook of Research on Curriculum* (pp. 327–344). New York: Macmillan.

Guthrie, J, Bennett, L and McGough, K (1994) *Concept-oriented reading instruction: an integrated curriculum to develop motivations and strategies for reading*, Reading Research Report No. 10. Georgia/Maryland: National Reading Research Center. This report is just one outcome of an extremely useful series of research projects led by John Guthrie at the University of Maryland. For more information about the CORI project, have a look at the website: **www.cori.umd.edu/overview/**

Guzzetti, B, Kowalinski, B and McGowan, T (1992) Using a literature-based approach to teaching social studies, *Journal of Reading*, 36 (2), pp. 114–122.

Hyland, K. (2000) *Disciplinary discourses: social interactions in academic writing.* Harlow: Pearson Education. This is a fascinating discussion of the differences in what counts as appropriate writing in a range of subject disciplines. Hyland is talking about 'academic' writing, of course. It is arguable how much this would apply to writing in the primary school, but his arguments should not be dismissed simply because of this issue.

Levstick, L (1990) Research directions: mediating content through literary texts, *Language Arts*, 67, pp. 848–853.

Lunzer, E and Gardner, K (1984) *Learning from the written word.* Oxford: Heinemann. This is dated now but is still one of the most useful accounts of approaches to developing the use of literacy across the curriculum at secondary school level in Britain.

Moore, S and Moore, D (1989) Literacy through content: content through literacy, *The Reading Teacher*, 42 (3), pp. 170–171.

Morrow, L, Pressley, M, Smith, J and Smith, M (1997) The effect of a literature-based program integrated into literacy and science instruction with children from diverse backgrounds, *Reading Research Quarterly*, 32 (1), pp. 54–76.

Palincsar, A and Herrenkohl, L (1999) Designing collaborative contexts: lessons from three research programs, in O'Donnell, A. and King, A. (eds) *Cognitive perspectives on peer learning* (pp. 151–178). Manwah, NJ: Lawrence Erlbaum.

Smith, J (1993) Content learning: a third reason for using literature in teaching reading, *Reading Research and Instruction*, 32 (3), pp. 64–71.

Smith, J, Monson, J and Dobson, D (1992) A case study on integrating history and reading instruction through literature, *Social Education*, 56 (7), pp. 370–375.

Traves, P (1994) Reading, in Brindley, S (ed.) *Teaching English*. London: Routledge/ Open University Press.

Winograd, K and Higgins, K (1995) Writing, reading and talking mathematics: one interdisciplinary possibility, *The Reading Teacher*, 48 (4), pp. 310–318.

Wray, D and Lewis, M (1997) *Extending literacy*. London: Routledge.

2 TEXT TYPES ACROSS THE PRIMARY CURRICULUM

Chapter objectives:

The aim of this chapter is to introduce you to:
* the concept of text type as a means of describing differences in what children are expected to read and write across the curriculum;
* the key differences between the various text types that children will encounter, in particular the non-fiction text types they meet in the various subjects of the curriculum.

Introduction

In the previous chapter I made the point that there are great differences between the kinds of texts readers and writers are likely to have to work with in different areas of the curriculum. If we are to help learners read and write effectively in these curriculum areas, it follows that we need to introduce them to the key features of the text types which they are likely to encounter.

When writers compose text, they generally organise that text around an internal structure or pattern. The texts that children encounter in school are usually either narratives or expositions – fiction or non-fiction. Narrative texts, or stories, chronicle events involving characters in a particular setting, while non-fiction texts generally seek to give information about, or explain, a phenomenon. Teaching children about text structure is one way to help them increase their understanding of the texts they read, both stories and non-fiction texts. It can also help them write more effectively in any of these genres. For example, if children expect a story to have a setting, characters, events and a conclusion, they will be able to fill those expectations with information unique to the particular story they are reading; the text's structure provides a framework to help them organise and remember the things they read about. When they come to write a story, they will be able to supply appropriate details to fit that framework and hence produce a more satisfying text.

The grammar of stories

Traditional grammar organises the structure of the sentences we use, and in a similar way story grammar describes the structures that are usually found in well-formed stories. According to Stein and Glenn (1977), a story basically consists of two parts: the setting plus one or more episodes. These two parts are what the story grammar describes.

Researchers into the structure of stories suggest that most of us have an expectation that a story will follow the structure shown below.

A typical story structure

1. Introduction of setting and character
2. An initiating event which sets a problem for the participating character(s)
3. The emotional response of the protagonist to that problem
4. The protagonist's actions to try to resolve the situation
5. The outcome of these actions and resolution of the problem
6. The reaction of the protagonist and others to the outcome

The setting introduces the main characters and outlines the time, place, and context in which the episodes occur. The initiating event allows the story to begin and sets up a possible or actual conflict. The protagonist reacts to that initiating event, which provides him/her with a goal that motivates subsequent action. There then follows action or a series of actions through which the protagonist attempts to attain the goal and resolve the conflict or problem. The consequences of these actions lead eventually to the resolution of the conflict or problem and the protagonists react to this resolution.

Story grammar research has consistently concluded that knowledge of story structure, albeit implicit knowledge, is critical to an understanding of stories. This knowledge seems to begin developing during the pre-school years and is refined throughout the primary school. Teachers can help this knowledge develop by providing many opportunities for children to experience stories – by reading aloud to them and providing plenty of books and opportunities for them to read.

It is established practice in most classrooms to discuss narrative forms with children. Teachers discuss the idea that stories have a beginning, a middle and an end, and they spend time working with children on, for example, alternative openings to stories such as 'Once upon a time', 'It was a dark and stormy night', 'Every day of the week', etc. They might analyse with children the traditional forms of fairy tales – exploring such features as the setting of a task, the quest undertaken by a hero, a 'chance' meeting with a stranger in need, and so on. They may discuss the vocabulary used in such a tale and how the events take place within a time frame. They conduct explicit discussions about these features with children by engaging in book talk and conferencing. They can also immerse children in the forms by reading them plenty of stories, by having a good supply of attractive story books in classrooms and by making strenuous efforts to 'sell' the books to children, including encouraging them to take books home.

Practical task

Mapping stories

Use the following 'story map', which is based on the story grammar analysis above, with some groups of children.

Mapping a story

What is the setting of the story (time, place)?

What characters are involved?

What is the main problem in the story?

How does the main character feel about the problem?

What does the character do to try to solve the problem?

How is the problem resolved?

How do the characters feel about this in the end?

Ask the children to think about a story they know well and to analyse it using the questions in the map. They might go on to do this with another story and then make comparisons. Later the story map could be used as a device for planning their own stories.

A focus on non-fiction

Although teachers may not have explicit command of the knowledge about story grammar we have just discussed, they do, as I have illustrated, have a range of ways of helping children come to an implicit understanding about the likely structures of stories. It is far less common, however, for teachers to discuss non-fiction texts in such ways.

One of the main reasons for this is that teachers, until fairly recently, have had little explicit knowledge of how various factual texts are organised. As competent language users we all implicitly 'know' how to write an explanation of why an event has happened and how the form of such writing differs from, say, that of a set of instructions. Yet we have generally lacked a shared vocabulary which would make talking about these written forms easy for us. The work of such researchers as Rothery (1985) and Martin (1985) has provided us with a way of making explicit our implicit knowledge about factual written forms and this work has been extended and embedded into a British context by Wray and Lewis (1997). The analysis we now have of the generic features of the main types of factual writing has given us a way to discuss such features with children.

Why is this important? Simply because, when we are thinking about literacy across the curriculum, the main text types which feature in lessons outside of the English subject area are non-fiction. Of course, it can be beneficial to include stories, and even poetry, in our teaching of science, history, mathematics, etc. I presented some evidence for the usefulness of that in the previous chapter. Nevertheless, for most children in these curriculum areas the kinds of texts they are going to be expected to read and write are non-fiction texts.

Practical task

The balance of text types

Look back at the information you collected in Practical task 1, 'Literacy shadowing', in the Introduction. Do a simple tally of the amount of fiction and non-fiction which your shadowed child(ren) read/wrote during the focus day.

What does this tally tell you about the relative prominence in a child's day of fiction and non-fiction?

You might also be able to glean from your data whether your children were more or less likely to be helped to read/write their fiction texts than their non-fiction. A hypothesis would be that because the reading/writing of non-fiction tends to serve a content-learning purpose rather than a literacy-learning purpose, children get less help from their teachers in reading/writing non-fiction texts.

If non-fiction texts are such a salient feature of children's literacy experiences across the curriculum, it seems important that teachers take steps deliberately to introduce them to the various structures of these texts. To do this, we need to explore what is commonly known now as 'genre theory'.

Genre theory

Genre theorists base their work on a functional approach to language. Such an approach looks at the ways in which language enables us to do things. It argues that we develop language to satisfy our needs in society. Based on Halliday's work (Halliday, 1975, 1978, 1985) on children's language, a functional language approach argues that as we use language several things happen. We:

- **learn language;**
- **learn through language;**
- **learn about language.**

We learn language by using language. If we think about our language development from our earliest years, we can see that we learn how to use language largely through using it. We refine and add to our vocabulary, for example, by constant exposure to other language users with whom we interact. As we get older we add to our knowledge of our language through reading and writing as well as through talking.

We also use language to interact with our world and increase our knowledge of it. We develop concepts, we ask questions, we make things happen through the medium of language. We learn *through* language.

As we use language we also acquire unconscious, implicit knowledge about how language itself works. Young children, for example, usually learn about plurals and begin to add an s to the ends of words in their speech long before they are formally 'taught' plurals in grammar lessons. Similarly, most children learn to distinguish between past and present tense in their language usage and use tenses appropriately before any formal instruction in this area. As we use language we learn *about* language. We now recognise that children come to school with an implicit knowledge of language structures and their usage.

A functional language approach argues that our implicit knowledge about language should be brought out into the open so that we can use it in our classrooms. One area of implicit knowledge that can be used in this way is our knowledge about genre.

What is 'genre'?

Over the last few years teachers have become aware of the term 'genre' as the work of certain teachers and academics has become more widely known. Just a few years ago, any of us asked to define genre would have probably replied in terms of book or film genres. We are all familiar with the idea that certain books or films have common characteristics which allow us to categorise them as 'romantic' or 'murder mysteries' or 'westerns' or 'horror' and so on. The genre theorists would argue that these are just a few of the many different genres that operate in our societies and that the term 'genre' can be applied to a much wider range of language-based activities. They see all texts, written and spoken, as being 'produced in response to, and out of, particular social situations and their specific structures' (Kress and Knapp, 1992, p. 5) and as a result put stress on the social and cultural factors that form a text as well as on its linguistic features. They see a text as always a social object and the making of a text as a 'social process' (ibid.). They argue that in any society there are certain types of text – both written and spoken – of a particular form because there are similar social encounters, situations and events which recur constantly within that society. As these 'events' are repeated over and over again, certain types of text are created over and over again. These texts become recognised in a society by its members, and once recognised they become conventionalised. If we take, for example, forms of greeting, we can see how this operates. If we meet an acquaintance in the street a common exchange might go as follows.

- *Hello. How are you?*
- *I'm fine thanks. How are you?*
- *Fine. Nice to see you. Bye.*
- *Bye.*

We all recognise this conventional type of exchange and implicitly 'know' the responses that are expected of us. We 'know' that we usually respond briefly and counter-question when queried about how we are. Yet nobody has ever explicitly taught us this text. We have learnt it through usage when similar purposes (acknowledging someone's presence without really getting involved in a conversation) for creating such a text have occurred. If our purpose were different (if, for example, we wanted to get involved in a more intimate conversation) we would structure our text in a different way. Our lives are full of such examples, when similar purposes and situations produce similar texts.

The genre theorists argue that texts have 'a high degree of internal structure' (Kress, 1982, p. 98) which largely remains invisible to the reader because when texts have become conventionalised (with recognisable rules and forms), they appear to have an existence of their own – they appear 'natural'. Genre theory looks at these larger textual structures of a whole text – what Kress calls the 'linguistic features beyond the sentence' (1982, p. 97) – as well as the language features within these larger structures.

Many genre theorists go on to argue that not only can we recognise generic structures but that the implicit knowledge we all have of generic structures should be made explicit and that knowledge of these forms and of their social meanings 'can and should be taught' (Kress and Knapp, p. 4).

Purpose and genre

Genre has been defined by many commentators. It is defined by some as being the structure found within a text, and commonly it is argued that the purpose of a text influences the form that text will take. Genre theory claims that texts (written or spoken) are structured according to their purposes, and texts with the same purpose will have the same schematic structure.

What does this idea of generic structures being determined by purpose actually mean? Let us take a written text type we are all familiar with – instructions. The purpose of instructions is to tell someone how to do something, as in recipes, instruction leaflets with machines, DIY leaflets and so on. This purpose gives rise to a particular form – instructions have to make clear what it is you are doing or making, what materials you need to achieve this aim, and the steps you need to take to reach a successful conclusion. It would not make it easier to achieve the purpose if, for example, the instructions were given first, then you were told the list of materials you needed at the end of the instructions and finally you were told what it was you were making. The schematic structure of a procedural text helps achieve its purpose and is therefore usually:

1. goal;
2. materials;
3. steps to achieve the goal (usually in temporal sequence).

You will be aware of such a structure in recipes and DIY guides. You may not have been explicitly aware of this structure but if you examine instruction ('how to') texts you will see that, on the whole, they follow the pattern outlined above. You will also be using a similar generic structure when you give any spoken instructions. If you imagine giving instructions to your class at the beginning of a session, you might say something like this.

1. *Today we're going to finish writing our stories.* (goal)

2. *So you'll need your jotters, pencils, line guides and best paper.* (materials)

3. *When you've got those sorted out, get on and see if you can finish your first draft. Then you can share it with your writing partner or with me and discuss any alterations you think need to be made. Don't forget to check spellings at the end. OK, off you go.* (instructions)

It is highly unlikely that you consciously planned to use, or were even aware of using, this schematic structure but your purpose (to tell the children what to do) meant that you 'automatically' used the appropriate structures – using such a structure came 'naturally'. When we look at how the schematic structure of a text helps it achieve its purpose, we are considering its genre.

Genre and culture

I said earlier that the creation of a text takes place within a culture or society. It is within a certain society that we have a purpose for creating a text and that purpose will give rise to a text produced in a particular genre. This means that if genres are formed within societies, they can vary from society to society even if the purpose is the same. A good example of this is the genre of shopping. The purpose of the language interchanges accompanying shopping within any society is to purchase goods and commodities. Within Western European society the generic structure of a shopping text would generally follow the form below.

1. mutual greeting   *Good morning.*

2. query   *Can I help you?*

3. shopping request   *I'd like . . .*

4. granting of request   *Certainly. What colour would you like . . .*

5. statement of price   *That will be . . .*

6. completing transaction   *Thank you. Goodbye.*

However, in different societies different norms are expected. There may, for instance, be an expectation that some bartering over the price will occur or that extended pleasantries will be expected before any mention of a transaction is broached. In these circumstances a different text with a different generic structure from the Western European model will be found. The purpose is the same, the genre is the same but the generic structure will be different. It is perhaps when we enter different societies that we become most aware of how 'learnt' the generic structures which we take for granted in our own society really are. We have all had experiences of situations where we have not 'known the script', say when ordering a meal in a foreign country, and we have been aware of making the wrong responses, getting the pace wrong and so on. We become aware that text structures are not automatic or natural but are learnt.

Written genres in the classroom

Different theorists have categorised the types of written genres we commonly use in the classroom in different ways. Collerson (1988), for example, suggests a separation into 'early' genres (labels, observational comment, recount, and narratives) and 'factual' genres (procedural, reports, explanations, and arguments or exposition), whereas Wing Jan (1991) categorises writing into 'factual' genres (reports, explanations, persuasive writing, etc.) and 'fictional' genres (traditional fiction and contemporary modern fiction).

There is, however, a large measure of agreement about the main non-fiction genres and the categories of non-fiction genres specified in the National Literacy Strategy are:

- **recount;**
- **report;**
- **procedure;**
- **explanation;**
- **exposition;**
- **discussion.**

Before looking at an analysis of these generic forms, I do need to stress that the idea of there being six main types of non-fiction genre does not mean that there are only six non-fiction genres in our society – there are many different genres and the possibility of new genres being created as new writing needs and media arise. There are also many examples of mixed genres.

Research insight

Non-fiction genres

The classification of non-fiction genres used in this book comes originally from the work of a group of linguists at Sydney University (Martin and Rothery, 1980, 1981, 1986). As part of their work this group collected and analysed non-fiction texts produced by adults in everyday life and by children in school. From this analysis they identified six important non-fiction genres which we use in our culture, and discovered that in school, one of these genres – the recount – was overwhelmingly predominant.

Interestingly, recounts were found quite rarely in adult writing (when did you last write to someone to tell them the story of what happened to you? Most of us use the telephone for that kind of event recounting). It seemed to be the case that the one genre which adults rarely use was the one which children were being given most practice of using in school.

The generic structures of factual texts

The basic concept underpinning genre theory is that the generic form of a text is determined by the purpose of that text. Purposes differ greatly and so each written genre has its own distinctive structural form and distinctive language features. Our knowledge of these structures and language features is largely implicit. The main purpose of the present chapter is to make some of this knowledge explicit. We will therefore look fairly closely at the main factual text types – recount, report, explanation, instructions, persuasion and discussion – to see what is known about the purpose, structure and language features of each of these genres. For each of these text types we will look at a typical example, using the writing of 8- to 10-year-old children, and then give information about the purpose, structure, typical language features, and common instances of this text type in everyday life.

TEXT A: a recount

Our trip to Exeter Museum

On Tuesday the 1st February we went on a school trip to a Roman museum in Exeter. First of all we split in to two groups. Then my group went upstairs. We looked at Roman tiles, bits of pottery, jawbones, a deer antler, a coin, sheep bone, and a bit of mosaic. We saw a tile which, before it was baked, a dog walked over and it had paw prints on it. When we went downstairs into the Roman kitchen which had been reconstructed from information from the ground. We did some observational drawings. Then we each had a turn at grinding the flour. The guide who took us around told us to look for a mysterious animal that the Romans ate. I was the first person to find out what it was. It was a hedgehog.

▶

Then we went to another museum. It was much better than the first because the man who took us round was funny and we were allowed to try on Roman armour. We handled the weapons as well. There was a sword, a dagger and a pilon. The armour was a breast plate, a shield, a helmet and a belt made with leather and chingles. The bits they hadn't got were the helmet, dagger and shield. Then we looked at a part of a mosaic. Then we went home.

It was a good trip. I liked the armour.

Factual text type	Recount	
Purpose	Recounts are written to retell events with the purpose of either informing or entertaining their audience (or even with both purposes).	
Structural features	The text opens with an orientation to the topic of the recount.	*Our trip to Exeter Museum* *On Tuesday ...*
	A list of events is given.	*First of all we ...*
	The text concludes with a reorientation to the topic and a comment.	*It was a good trip. I ...*
Language features	The text features personal participants, that is, it is about somebody or something in particular.	*we, my group*
	It uses mainly chronological connectives.	*then, first*
	The past tense is used, as these are events that have already happened.	*we went, we looked*
Instances in everyday life	Recounts are often found in biographies, autobiographies and history texts.	

TEXT B: a report

Lungs

Our lungs are organs in our body which do the breathing.
The lungs are divided into sections called lobes. There are two lobes in the left lung, and three lobes in the right lung. Inside each lobe, the lung tubes split and split again, and soon look like this:

[Here Simon had drawn a diagram]

At the end of the lung is a 'bubble' called an alveolus. When we breathe in, the oxygen enters our blood via the alveoli, and when we breathe out, the carbon dioxide leaves us in the same way. When we smoke, the alveoli get clogged up with tar, so we cannot breathe properly.

Factual text type	Report	
Purpose	Reports are written to describe the way things are. They can describe a range of natural, cultural or social phenomena.	
Structural features	The text opens with a general classifying statement about the topic of the report.	**Lungs** *Our lungs are …*
	A description of the phenomenon follows.	*The lungs are divided …*
Language features	The text features generic participants, that is, it is about a general phenomenon.	*lungs, the oxygen* (not one specific set of lungs, and not any particular mass of oxygen)
	It uses mainly conditional and logical connectives.	*when, so*
	The present tense is used, as these are timeless events.	*when we breathe, the alveoli get clogged up*
Instances in everyday life	Reports are often found in science and geography textbooks and in encyclopedias.	

TEXT C: an explanation

The water cycle

The water cycle is about what happens to water. I want to explain where rain comes from.

To begin with the sun shines on the sea and turns it into water vapour and the water vapour rises up into the sky. Next the wind blows it and it turns into clouds. Then as it gets colder the water vapour condenses back into water. This falls as rain. It runs down the hills and under the earth and into the rivers and seas. Finally it starts again.

Factual text type	Explanation	
Purpose	Explanations are written to advance a set of reasons underpinning a phenomenon (to say 'why' or 'how').	
Structural features	The text opens with a general statement about the phenomenon to be explained.	*The water cycle* *The water cycle is …*
	There then follows a series of steps explaining the phenomenon.	*To begin with the sun shines …*
Language features	The text features generic participants, that is, it is about a general phenomenon.	*the sun, rain*
	It uses chronological connectives (logical connectives are also often used, although not in this case).	*to begin with, next*
	The present tense is used.	*the sun shines, the wind blows*
Instances in everyday life	Explanations are often found in science, geography, history and social science textbooks. They are often embedded within other text types, such as reports.	

TEXT D: a set of instructions

Object of game

The object of the game is to get to the finish with all of the items.

Equipment

For the game you will need: 1 die, 2–4 counters, the 15 item cards.

How to play

1. Each player chooses a counter and the person who throws a six first starts.
2. After you have thrown the die, move the number spaces it says on it.
3. If you land on a shop, pick up one item card. If not, carry on. If you land on a space which says lose something, place the item it says in the lost item space.
4. If you have not got all the cards by the time you have got to the finish, keep going round until you have got them. This game is for two to four players.

Factual text type	Instructions	
Purpose	Instructions are written to describe how something is done through a series of sequenced steps.	
Structural features	Opens with a statement of the goal of these instructions.	**Object of game** *The object of the game is …*
	A list of equipment needed (ingredients) is given.	**Equipment** *For the game you will need …*
	There then follows a list of steps to achieve the goal.	**How to play** *1. Each player …*
Language features	The text features generic participants – it is aimed at no one person in particular.	*you, each player*
	Chronological and conditional connectives are used.	*after, if*
	The imperative or command form of the verb is used.	*move, pick up*
Instances in everyday life	Instructions are commonly found in instruction manuals, with games, and in recipe books.	

TEXT E: persuasion

Should houses be built on the old school field?

I think that building houses on the old school field is a bad thing. I have several reasons for thinking this like the wildlife and the Youth Club.

My first reason is that it would be destroying wildlife on the field because of all the digging and when the people move in the noise, the light and other things.

A further reason is the Youth Club would not like it because they use the field for games and other things. And they might disturb the people in the houses. Furthermore there are enough houses in the village. We do not need any more. It would just be a waste of space. (We need that space.)

Therefore although some people think it would be a good thing to because it would create more homes I think I have shown lots of reasons why it is not a very good idea to build more houses here especially on the old school field.

Factual text type	Persuasion	
Purpose	Persuasive writing takes many forms from advertising copy to polemical pamphlets but its purpose is to try to promote a particular point of view or argument – unlike a discussion paper which considers different points of view.	
Structural features	Opens with a statement of the point of view to which the writer will try to persuade the reader.	*I think that …*
	A number of points are put forward in the argument. Each point is elaborated upon.	*My first reason is that …*
	Concludes with a reiteration of the thesis of the text.	*Therefore although some people think …*
Language features	The text features largely generic participants.	*wildlife, some people*
	Logical connectives predominate.	*therefore, because*
	The simple present tense is most commonly used, although conditionals also feature (would).	*some people think, we do not need*
Instances in everyday life	Persuasive writing is found in pamphlets and booklets produced by special-interest groups, in political writing, in publicity and promotional material.	

TEXT F: discussion

The issue I would like to discuss is whether smoking is bad for you. Some people think that it is alright to smoke but other people say that it is bad for your health.

Some people think that smoking is enjoyable. They like having cigarettes. They say it makes you look cool and that it helps you to concentrate on things better. Children think it is cool when they see their friends and parents smoke and they see children on films and TV programmes smoking.

Children smoke so that they look older and so they can get into pubs and clubs.

Other people think that it gives you heart disease and lung cancer, and it damages your health. When a lady is pregnant, it could kill her baby.

Smoking makes you smell horrible and some people say it can lead to drugs. It is a habit you can't get out of and it's a waste of money. If people fall asleep when they are smoking it could cause a fire.

I think that because there are more arguments against it is better not to smoke.

Factual text type	Discussion	
Purpose	Discussion papers are written to present arguments and information from differing viewpoints before reaching a conclusion based on the evidence.	
Structural features	Opens with a statement of the issue to be discussed.	*The issue I would like to discuss is . . .*
	A list of points in favour of the issue is presented.	*Some people think that smoking is . . .*
	This is followed by a list of points against the issue.	*Other people think that . . .*
	The writing concludes with a recommendation.	*I think that . . .*
Language features	Generic participants predominate.	*some people, children*
	Logical, not chronological, connectives link ideas together.	*so that, but, if*
	The present tense predominates, although some conditionals also feature.	*think, say*
Instances in everyday life	Discussions are often found in philosophical texts, history and social study texts, newspaper editorials.	

Summary

These analyses of generic structures and their language features are useful in that they give us the knowledge and vocabulary to discuss factual genres with our children in the same way that we explicitly discuss narrative genres with them.

Of course, not all, or even most, texts will be found in the 'pure' form in which they have just been analysed. Most texts will, in fact, contain a mixture of genres. For example, reports often include a section containing an explanation; a recount may well be interspersed with elements of report and description. Real-life texts do not always to conform perfectly to the analysis we have just shown. This analysis should be read as providing general guiding principles. Just as skilled writers play around with the story genre — perhaps starting with the ending, or deliberately writing a story in a factual genre such as a mock police report, for example — so factual genres can be mixed, played around with, parodied. The analyses are given as an aid to understanding a genre, not as a straitjacket, demanding rigid adherence.

Furthermore, these analyses should not be seen as an invitation to move into formal lessons with children on text types and structures. This knowledge can be used, however, to ensure that our classrooms contain the full range of factual texts so that the children experience books, pamphlets, letters and documents of all kinds written in a variety of genres.

We also need to read aloud to children from this wide range of factual texts as well as from fiction texts because we need to help them become familiar with the structures, patterns and rhythms of all texts. This 'immersion' is important. As Margaret Meek (1988, p. 21) puts it, 'The most important single lesson that children learn from texts is the nature and variety of written discourse, the different ways that language lets a writer tell, and the many different ways a reader reads.' This is as important for factual as for fiction texts.

References and further reading

Collerson, J (ed.) (1988) *Writing for life*. New South Wales: Primary English Teaching Association.

Halliday, MAK (1975) *Learning how to mean: explorations in the development of language*. London: Arnold.

Halliday, MAK (1978) *Language as a social semiotic: The theoretical interpretation of language and meaning*. London: Arnold.

Halliday, MAK (1985) *An introduction to functional grammar*. London: Arnold.

Kress, G (1982) *Learning to write*. London: Routledge.

Kress, G and Knapp, P (1992) Genre in a social theory of language, *English in Education*, 26 (2).

Lewis, M and Wray, D (1995) *Developing children's non-fiction writing*. Leamington Spa: Scholastic. This book contains a rather more detailed version of the analysis of non-fiction text types which appears in this chapter. It also contains a full discussion of the theory behind and the use of writing frames to help teach the writing of these text types.

Martin, J (1985) *Factual writing: exploring and challenging social reality.* Oxford: Oxford University Press. Quite a challenging but very influential text which really pulls apart the nature of the non-fiction writing that typically gets written in school contexts. Introduced the functional linguistic analysis of texts which has been at the core of the movement towards genres in the teaching of writing.

Martin, JR and Rothery, J (1980) *Writing Project Report No. 1.* Department of Linguistics. Sydney: University of Sydney.

Martin, JR and Rothery, J (1981) *Writing Project Report No. 2.* Department of Linguistics. Sydney: University of Sydney.

Martin, JR and Rothery, J (1986) *Writing Project Report No. 4.* Department of Linguistics. Sydney: University of Sydney.

Meek, M (1988) *How texts teach what readers learn.* Stroud: Signal.

Rothery, J (1985) *Teaching writing in the primary school: a genre-based approach to the development of writing abilities.* Department of Linguistics. Sydney: University of Sydney.

Stein, N and Glenn, C (1977) An analysis of story comprehension in elementary school children, in R. Freedle (ed.) *New directions in discourse processing: Vol. 2, Advances in discourse processing.* Hillsdale, NJ: Ablex.

Wing Jan, L (1991) *Write ways. Modelling writing forms.* Melbourne: Oxford University Press.

Wray, D and Lewis, M (1997) *Extending literacy.* London: Routledge.

3 TEACHING NON-FICTION READING

Chapter objectives:

The aim of this chapter is to introduce you to:
- some of the problems that children may find as they read for information and learning across the curriculum;
- a number of approaches to avoiding the wholesale copying which often characterises children's use of non-fiction texts;
- a teaching model for introducing these strategies to young learners.

Introduction

Zoë is a 10-year-old with reading difficulties. Her class is currently studying 'Living things' as their topic in science. For this lesson Zoë and her group have been asked to choose a particular living thing which interests them and to 'find out about it'. Zoë and her friends have chosen dolphins and have picked out several information books from their class collection. For the next 45 minutes or so they work quietly and diligently with these books.

Towards the end of the lesson Zoë's support teacher arrives and goes to check on what the girls have done. In Zoë's book she finds the piece of writing shown on page 29 (Figure 3.1).

Most teachers will recognise what has happened here. Zoë has copied, word for word, from one or more information books. The teacher asks Zoë to read out what she has written but Zoë finds this nearly impossible to do. She also asks Zoë what she thinks she has learnt about dolphins, but Zoë cannot really think of much. She has not processed what she has written beyond simply recognising that it is about dolphins. She has learnt very little from the lesson.

Research (e.g. Wray and Lewis, 1992) suggests that most primary children know quite well that they should not copy directly from information books. Many children can give good reasons for this. Eight-year-old Anna, for example, claimed that 'you learn a lot more if you write it in your own words'. Yet, when faced with the activity of finding out from books, most children at some stage resort to copying. Why is this so common and how can teachers help children read for information more effectively?

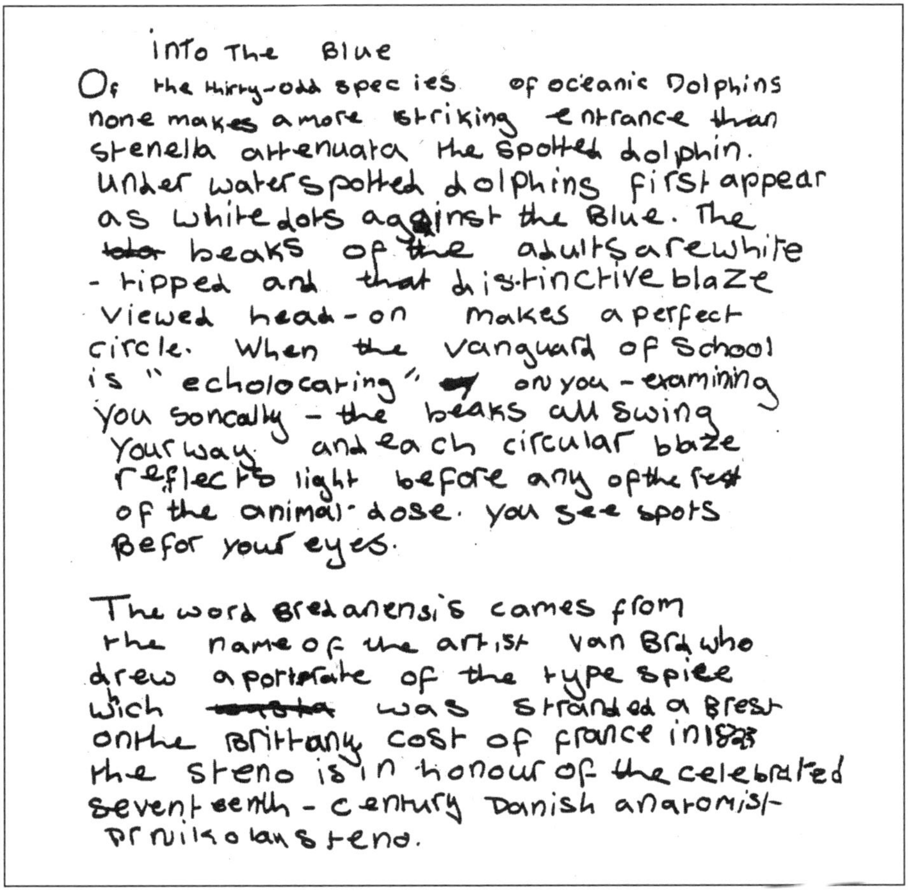

> into The Blue
>
> Of the thirty-odd species of oceanic Dolphins none makes a more striking entrance than stenella attenuata the spotted dolphin. Under water spotted dolphins first appear as white dots against the Blue. The ~~color~~ beaks of ~~the~~ adults are white - tipped and ~~that~~ distinctive blaze viewed head-on makes a perfect circle. When ~~the~~ vanguard of School is "echolocating" ~~of~~ on you - examining you soncally - the beaks all swing your way and each circular blaze reflects light before any of the rest of the animal-close. you see spots Befor your eyes.
>
> The word Bredanensis comes from the name of the artist van Brd who drew a portraite of the type spice wich ~~was sto~~ was stranded a Brest on the Brittany cost of France in 1833 the steno is in honour of the celebrated seventeenth - century Danish anatomist Dr Nils olaus steno.

Figure 3.1 Zoë's writing about dolphins

Practical task

Why do children copy?

Discuss the issue of copying with a group of children you work with. You might focus your discussion around the following questions:

- *Is it OK to copy from information books?*

- *Why is it/isn't it OK?*

- *Have you ever copied material from a book?*

- *Why did you do this?*

- *Did it help you learn the material you were copying?*

- *What do you think you can do rather than copy from the books?*

The task and the text

One important part of the problem seems to be the nature of the task children are often given when using information books. Zoë's task of 'finding out about' a topic is a common one but one which is not very helpful in focusing her on understanding what she finds. If the task is to find out about dolphins, then presumably any information about dolphins is acceptable. As Zoë discovers, there are whole books full of information about dolphins. How can she choose among all this information? She has no way of narrowing down the task and it becomes unmanageable. She really needs help before looking in the books in deciding what she wants to find out about dolphins.

Even if children manage to use 'information-retrieval skills' well enough to locate material on the required topic, they still often find the text in that material difficult to deal with. Children in primary classrooms tend to lack experience of the different genres of non-fiction and their organisational structures (Littlefair, 1991). They find the linguistic features (vocabulary, connectives, cohesion, register) more difficult to comprehend than those of the more familiar narrative texts. Most children need support from teachers to enable them to cope more easily with the problems of factual text. There are a number of teaching strategies which can provide this support and make the activity of reading information a much more purposeful one.

What do I know and what do I want to know?

Zoë's support teacher did not leave things as they were. She was due to spend a lesson working with Zoë, so she decided to introduce a different way of approaching the task. At the end of the lesson Zoë had produced a very different piece of writing about dolphins (see Figure 3.2).

How had the support teacher moved Zoë on from passive copying to what appears to be a more thoughtful extension of her understanding about this topic?

The first step was to close the information books Zoë had been using. In teaching children to read non-fiction texts for understanding, an important part of the process occurs before the eyes meet the page. The teacher asked Zoë to think about two of the most crucial questions in any experience of reading for information.

- **What do I already know about this topic?**
- **What do I want to know about it?**

How thay live.
Dolphins live in familys and oftern there is
about 7 in a family. There would Be about
3 femails in one Family But only one
femail.

I Dolphin live for aBout 25 years
But pillot wales can live por 50
years. Killer whales have Been known
ro live longer.

Sometimes Dolphins get whashed
onto the Beach which means that
there skin BoDys get hot and
unless thay are helped Back
into the water thay Shall Die
even if thay are helped thay
make there way Back to
help other Dolphins. Thay make
there way Back to help Because
thay hear the Distresing cry
of other Dolphins. We Donot
know why thay Do this.

Figure 3.2 *Zoë's second piece of writing about dolphins*

The importance of the first of these questions is that understanding is built upon the schemas (or pre-existing structures of knowledge) already in the learner's mind. But we carry around a multitude of schemas. What has to happen when we read is that somehow the appropriate schemas are triggered before we approach the texts. For accomplished readers, this can be an automatic process – we see the title of a text, and that immediately brings into our minds information we already know that will help us in subsequent understanding. Less expert readers may need some help in this triggering, and their teachers can actively help them access relevant previous knowledge.

Many teachers use discussion to activate previous knowledge but there are a range of other approaches to this which have the added advantage of giving the teacher some record of what children seem to know about a particular topic. One especially useful device is the KWL grid. This is a simple but effective strategy which both takes children through the steps of the research process and also records their learning. A KWL grid consists of three columns (see Figure 3.3).

What do I KNOW about this topic	What do I WANT to know?	What have I LEARNT?

Figure 3.3 *A KWL grid*

Zoë's support teacher introduced her to the strategy by drawing a KWL grid as three columns in Zoë's book. She then asked Zoë what she already knew about dolphins and acted as a scribe to record Zoë's responses. What Zoë knew can be seen in the first column of Figure 3.4. In the introductory stages of teaching the strategy, as for most new strategies and skills, teacher modelling is very important. Only when the child is thoroughly familiar with the strategy should they be encouraged to attempt it independently.

What I Know

clever/smart
favourite food · squid
related to whale
live in the sea
hunted by fishermen
beautiful

What I want to find out

how they live p18
where they live
why do people hunt them

Figure 3.4 *Zoë's KWL grid*

Not only did this tapping into previous knowledge have a vital role to play in helping Zoë comprehend the texts she was to read, but it also gave her an active role in the topic right from the beginning. By asking her what she knew, her self-esteem and sense of 'ownership' of knowledge were enhanced instead of her being faced instantly with the (for her) negative experience of tackling a text without knowing quite how she was to make sense of it.

The next stage was to help Zoë establish some purposes for her reading by asking her what she wanted to know now. This was aimed at helping to focus her subsequent reading. What Zoë had originally been asked to do ('find out about dolphins'), although a very common way of approaching this kind of task, is actually far too broad to be useful. How could Zoë answer this? There are books full of information about dolphins so she could, perhaps, be forgiven for thinking that the real purpose of the task she had been set was for her to accumulate as much information as she could, rather than understand what she read.

This time, the discussion and the recording of what she already knew was enough to generate further questions for Zoë – questions which she would be interested in researching. These were again scribed by the teacher (see the second column of Figure 3.4).

In this case Zoë generated her own questions, but when children find this difficult there are a number of question-setting strategies that can be used.

- **Turning 'what I know' statements into questions, e.g. 'Whales are hunted by fishermen' can become, 'Why are whales hunted by fishermen?'**
- **Introducing them to the six question words, *what, where, when, why, who, how.***
- **Using various graphic forms to add child appeal, e.g. question trees, question hands, question wheels with questions on each branch, finger, spoke.**

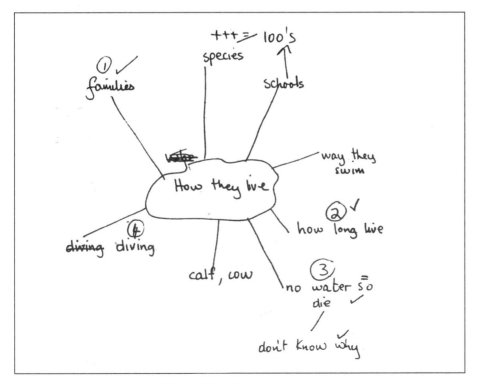

Figure 3.5 *Zoë's concept map*

On this occasion Zoë and her teacher decided to concentrate on just one question (they had only an hour together) and she was encouraged to brainstorm around her 'How do they live?' question. Again her teacher scribed and the resultant concept map can be seen in Figure 3.5.

The sub-questions generated by this were numbered to keep the process clear and manageable. At this point Zoë was ready to return to her information books to try to find the answers to her questions. Now Zoë also had key words which she could use to search the index/contents, etc. Sometimes her teacher wrote the word on a piece of card for her so that she could run it down the index/page and match the word. This gave her practice in scanning. We can see from the writing she had completed by the end of the session (Figure 3.2) that she was working her way logically through the questions (she had completed 1 and 2) and not only had she learnt something about dolphins but she had also had a powerful lesson on how to set about reading for information.

Effective reading strategies

What the above case study of Zoë's work illustrates is that, through the teaching of some relatively simple strategies for understanding text, it is possible to move on children's use of information text considerably. There are a number of such strategies which have proved useful and I will describe and illustrate some of these in the following chapter. You should also bear in mind that, increasingly, children gather information not from books but from electronic information sources such as CD-ROMs and the internet. Teaching them strategies to handle such a bewildering array of information is even more important. I will make some suggestions about this aspect of literacy across the curriculum in a later chapter. In the remainder of the present chapter, I will discuss an approach to teaching children to use such reading strategies, and present a teaching model.

Research insight

Teaching reading strategies

Grabe and Stoller (2002) provide a comprehensive review of research into reading development which strongly suggests that good readers use strategies that are not used by poorer readers. Research also suggests that children learning to read can and need to be taught how to use specific strategies for understanding a text. There seems to be no support in the research for the traditional approach of schools to this issue – that is, if children are good basic readers they will learn by themselves how to use their reading as a tool for learning. Instead, it seems to be the case that readers need explicit teaching and plenty of guided practice if reading strategy training is to be successful. Essential components of this teaching seem to be that the teacher explains what the strategy is, why it should be learned, and how, when, and where the strategy should be used.

A teaching model for developing non-fiction reading

The model of teaching and developing reading across the curriculum that is best supported by research includes a number of teaching components. Each of these is essential if readers are to be given full control of the ways in which they can use reading as a means of learning. These teaching components are listed in the approximate order in which they would be used, although there is always scope for some flexibility in this.

1. An explicit description of the strategy and when it should be used

Learners need first of all to have a clear picture in their minds of what they are going to be asked to do in a particular strategy. As we will see later when we go on to discuss approaches to teaching writing across the curriculum, this element of learners getting clear in their minds the nature of the activity/skills they are going to be learning is a crucial element of any effective skill learning. After all, you could never have learnt to ride a bicycle unless you knew what riding a bicycle involved. Just looking at the machine itself would not have given you sufficient information: you needed to know what the various pieces did – how pedals worked, how the handlebars helped you steer, etc. Such understanding of the key elements of a skill has been called 'cognitive clarity' and there is plenty of research to suggest it is an essential element in effective skill learning.

Research insight

Cognitive clarity and the learning of literacy

In a book published in 1994 (Wray, 1994), I did a thorough review of the research up to that date into the relationship between what has been called 'cognitive clarity' and the development of literacy. The terms I used then were 'metalinguistic' or 'metacognitive awareness'. I concluded this review with the statement, 'There is ample evidence that there is a close relationship between skilful and appropriate use of literacy and a well developed awareness of its purposes, its strategies and one's own competence in these.' Research carried out since 1994 has confirmed this relationship (e.g. Lazo et al., 1997; Bialystok, 2001).

One way of helping learners develop such clarity is by clearly explaining the strategy involved, its purpose and when it might be used. Look at the following example of a teacher explaining the prediction strategy.

Predicting is making guesses about what will come next in the text you are reading. Good readers make predictions a lot when they read and this helps them to understand what they are reading. Good times to make predictions are when a new character is first introduced into a story, or when a main character has a problem that will need to be solved. At points like these, you might stop reading for a short time and think. What is this new character likely to be like or do in the story? How might the problem be solved? What might happen next? Then you read on to check whether your predictions were right or not.

2. Teacher modelling of the strategy in action

Children also need to see the strategy applied by an expert reader so that they can see how it helps understanding. The most expert reader in the class is usually the teacher, but there is no reason why, occasionally, children themselves should not model the process (this swapping of roles between teacher and children is part of the reciprocal teaching procedure, which we will discuss in the next chapter). Here is an example of one teacher modelling her reading of a story. (An example of this kind of 'teacher think-aloud' using a non-fiction text will be given in the next chapter.)

> I am going to make predictions while I read this book. I'll start by looking at the cover. Hmm . . . the picture is of a small boat, filled with people, sailing in a very rough sea. It looks as if they may have been shipwrecked so perhaps the story will have something to do with this wreck and what happens to the survivors afterwards.
>
> The title will give me more clues about the book; the title is Sea of Peril. So this makes me think even more that this book is going to be about a shipwreck.
>
> Okay, I've made some predictions about the book based on the front cover. Now I'm going to look at the back cover and read what is written there. This is usually called the 'blurb', and it gives me some important clues about the plot of the book.

Practical task

Modelling reading

Use the strategy-modelling approach described above to carry out a shared reading activity with some children using a non-fiction text. You should plan this activity to be part of a subject lesson other than literacy, so the text you choose should fit with the content you want the children to learn in this subject.

As always in shared reading, you will need to work on a text which is clearly visible to all of the children in the group, using either an overhead projector or an electronic whiteboard as your display mechanism.

3. Collaborative use of the strategy in action

If the strategy has been modelled, the children can then go on to try it out for themselves. This initial trial will work best if they are given very close support, so a collaborative approach, with the teacher working closely alongside the class or group, will be needed. Few children will be able to use a strategy independently after simply seeing it used a couple of times by someone else. They need more guided practice than that.

I've made some good predictions so far about this book. From now on I want you to make predictions with me. We'll read a page or so together and then each of us will stop and think about what might happen next … Okay, now let's hear what you think and why …

4. Guided practice using the strategy with gradual transference of responsibility from teacher to child

Children need to be given practice in applying the strategy. Some will be able to do this independently more or less straight away; others will need more guidance. The purpose of this guidance is to gradually wean them off the support given by the teacher, until they are able to take more and more of the responsibility themselves.

Guidance given early on in this process might be something like the following:

I've called this group together to work on making predictions while you read this text. After every few paragraphs I will ask each of you to stop and make a prediction. We will talk about your predictions and then read on to see if they come true.

Later on the guidance might be less teacher-focused:

Each of you has a chart that lists different paragraphs in this text. When you finish reading a paragraph on the list, stop and make a prediction. Write the prediction in the column that says 'Prediction'. When you get to the next paragraph on the list, check whether your prediction 'Happened', 'Will not happen', or 'Still might happen'. Then make another prediction and write that down.

5. Children's independent use of the strategy

It's time for silent reading. As you read today, remember what we've been working on – making predictions while we read. Be sure to make predictions every two or three paragraphs. Ask yourself why you made the prediction you did – what made you think that. Check as you read to see whether or not your prediction came true.

At least some of the texts used during these different phases of strategy teaching should be chosen to be particularly well suited to the application of the specific strategy being learnt. You will also need to pay careful attention to the level and demands of the texts used at different phases of the teaching, especially early on. When children are first learning a comprehension strategy, they should use texts that do not make heavy demands in other respects, such as background knowledge, vocabulary difficulty, etc. Later, of course, children must be asked to apply the strategy to the range of texts they will meet during their normal classwork, and their reading outside of school.

Finally, as with any good teaching, teaching comprehension strategies should be accompanied by ongoing assessment. You will need to monitor your children's use of comprehension strategies and their success at understanding what they read. The results of this monitoring should, in turn, inform your subsequent approach. When a particular strategy continues to be used ineffectively, or not at all, you should respond with additional teaching or a fresh approach to the teaching. At the same time, children should be monitoring their own use of comprehension strategies, aware of their strengths as well as their weaknesses as developing understanders of text.

Summary

The aim of this chapter has been to suggest that problems often emerge when children are asked to read to learn in curriculum areas outside English and literacy. In particular, many children will resort to simply copying out large portions of the subject texts they encounter, benefiting neither their reading skills nor their knowledge and understanding of the subject matter of these texts. There are, however, steps you can take as a teacher to minimise such copying, steps which principally involve teaching children a range of reading strategies which may be new to them. This chapter has discussed an approach to introducing such strategies. In the following chapter, I will present and illustrate a range of strategies which children will find useful in their reading across the curriculum.

References and further reading

Bialystok, E (2001) *Bilingualism in development. Language, literacy, and cognition.* Cambridge: Cambridge University Press.

Grabe, W and Stoller, F (2002) *Teaching and researching reading*. Harlow: Pearson Education.

Lazo, M, Pumfrey, P and Peers, I (1997) Metalinguistic awareness, reading and spelling: roots and branches of literacy, *Journal of Research in Reading*, 20 (2), pp. 85–104.

Littlefair, A (1991) *Reading all types of writing*. Buckingham: Open University Press. This is a very important, and readable, book, which was the first to introduce the ideas of the Australian genre theorists to an audience of British teachers. Littlefair gives a detailed and useful analysis not just of the concept of text type but also of the registers which are associated with different types of communication.

Wray, D (1994) *Literacy and awareness*. London: Hodder & Stoughton. This book presents a full review of the existing literature on the importance of metalinguistic awareness to the development of language and literacy. The book is written in a practical way to include many suggestions for teaching responses to this literature.

Wray, D and Lewis, M (1992) Primary children's use of information books, *Reading*, 26 (3), pp. 19–24.

4 STRATEGIES FOR NON-FICTION READING

Chapter objectives:

The aim of this chapter is to introduce you to:
- *a range of strategies that readers can use to help them make sense of the non-fiction texts they read across the curriculum;*
- *some practical examples of the use of these strategies with young learners.*

Introduction

In the previous chapter, I explored the ways in which children's reading across the curriculum can be developed and enhanced by the teaching of a range of comprehension strategies. In this chapter, I will describe and illustrate a number of such strategies: strategies which have been found in research to have a positive effect on children's achievement as they read to learn. That is, not only do they enhance children's abilities to read effectively, they also help them to learn subject material more effectively – a real win–win situation.

Strategy 1: Prediction

Prediction is better thought of as a family of strategies rather than a single strategy. At its core, it involves the reader in making predictions and then reading to see how these turn out, but it can also involve activities such as activating prior knowledge, previewing and overviewing. What all of these activities have in common is that they encourage children to use their existing knowledge to help their understanding of new ideas encountered in text. These activities are based upon the idea that comprehension is the bridge between the known and the new.

Most of the research into the effectiveness of the prediction strategy has involved narrative texts. Activities which have been shown to be effective in enhancing comprehension include the following.

- **Encouraging children to predict what characters in a story might do based upon their own experiences in similar situations.**
- **Getting children to compose very short narratives based upon a list of key words from a story which they would go on to study. For example, *loose tooth, string, pain, football match, tense draw* and *last-minute winner* might serve as key words for a story about a boy with a loose tooth that will not come out but that falls out naturally when he is engrossed in a very close football match.**
- **Explicitly comparing child predictions about the outcomes of a story with the actual unfolding events.**

Prediction can also successfully be used with information texts. An example of this is given in Practical task 4.1 below using the history text, 'How did William the Conqueror get control of England?' given in Figure 4.1. The best way to use this text is to make an overhead transparency of it and show it using a projector.

How did William the Conqueror get control of England?

After the Battle of Hastings, William had to take control of his new kingdom. This was not an easy task.

First William marched to London, burning the countryside in order to warn people that it was not worth fighting him. The Witan, who were the English leaders, surrendered to him. He was crowned King of England on Christmas Day, 1066.

However, this was not the end of the resistance William encountered. William had to crush many rebellions. He was ruthless and reacted harshly to any opposition.

One example of this took place in 1069–70 and is known as the Harrying of the North. William destroyed large areas of land, usually by burning. Because no crops would grow, people had nothing to eat. Thousands of people died of cold and hunger. One source, Simeon of Durham, wrote that the destruction or harrying was so harsh that 'there was no village inhabited between York and Durham'.

So that he could keep control, William built many motte and bailey castles. Taking less than 10 days to build, they were initially made of wood. These were later replaced by stone. The castles were placed outside Saxon towns in order to deter uprisings. Gradually, areas around the castles became peaceful.

Figure 4.1 *A sample text for prediction*

Practical task

A prediction activity

1. *Begin by showing the class the title of the passage and discussing it with them. How did William get control of England after the Battle of Hastings? Ask children for any suggestions they can make about what the rest of the passage is likely to tell them.*

2. *Show them the first paragraph of the text: After the Battle of Hastings William had to take control of his new kingdom. This was not an easy task. Discuss with them why it was not an easy task and what William might have done. Ask them to predict what William did first.*

3. *Show them the next paragraph of the text: First William marched to London, burning the countryside ... Was this the end of the matter? What happened next and how did William respond to this?*

4. *Show them the next paragraph of the text: However, this was not the end of the resistance ... Continue the discussion about William's likely actions. What might the next paragraph tell us?*

5. *Carry on in a similar way to the end of the text.*

Strategy 2: Think-alouds

'Think-alouds' involve making one's thoughts audible and, usually, public – saying what you are thinking while you are performing a task, in this case, reading. The use of think-alouds has been shown to improve children's comprehension both when children themselves engage in the practice during reading and also when teachers routinely think aloud while reading to children.

Teacher think-alouds

Teacher think-alouds are a form of teacher modelling. By thinking aloud, teachers demonstrate effective comprehension strategies and, at least as importantly, when and when not to apply them. As an example of this teaching strategy, here is an extract from some classroom discussion. The class were examining a non-narrative text on the topic of 'Engines' and the teacher began by sharing a photocopied extract from the book with them. She accompanied her reading of this text by a commentary explaining her thinking as she worked with its ideas. Here is the first part of her reading (the words in italics are directly read from the text):

Now, this passage is called *The Steam Engine*. I hope it might tell me something about how steam engines work and perhaps about how they were invented. I know that James Watt made the first steam engine. I suppose the passage might tell me when this happened. I'll read the first sentence or so. *The power developed by steam has fascinated people for hundreds of years. During the first century AD, Greek scientists realised that steam contained energy that could possibly be used by people.* Oh, it looks like the power of steam has been known about for longer than I thought. *The first century AD –* that's around 1900 years ago. I'm not sure what it means about steam containing energy though. I'd better read carefully to try to find that out.

Figure 4.2 *An example of think-aloud*

During this reading, the teacher was concentrating on doing four kinds of things. She was:

- **predicting, looking forward to the information the text might give her;**
- **clarifying, working out ideas in ways she could better understand them;**
- **questioning, allowing the text to spark off further questions in her mind;**
- **summarising, putting the information in the text into a few words.**

Research studies have suggested that this kind of teacher modelling is most effective when it is explicit, leaving the child to infer little about the strategy and its application; and flexible, adjusting the use of the strategy to the text rather than presenting it as a set of rigid rules.

Child think-alouds

Inviting children themselves to think aloud as they are reading has also been shown to be effective at improving comprehension. It appears that getting children to think aloud as they read tends to prevent them impulsively jumping to decisions about the meanings they are encountering. Rather than jumping to conclusions about text meaning or moving ahead in the text without having sufficiently understood what has already been read, think-alouds may lead to more thoughtful, strategic reading.

Research insight

Research on think-alouds

1. *Baumann, JF, Jones, LA and Seifert-Kessell, N (1993) Using think alouds to enhance children's comprehension monitoring abilities,* **The Reading Teacher,** *47 (3), pp. 184–193.*

This article describes and evaluates the use of think-alouds in teaching reading. The researchers conclude that teaching children how to think aloud helps them to monitor their own comprehension and to determine what to do if they do not understand what they are reading.

2. *Kucan, L and Beck, IL (1997) Thinking aloud and reading comprehension research: Inquiry, instruction, and social interaction,* **Review of Educational Research,** *67 (3), pp. 271–299.*

This article reviews research that considers think-alouds as a means of teaching and encouraging social interaction in the classroom. The review demonstrates that think-alouds can be a very successful method of teaching reading comprehension.

3. *Loxterman, JA, Beck, IL and McKeown, MG (1994) The effects of thinking aloud during reading on students' comprehension of more or less coherent text,* **Reading Research Quarterly,** *29 (4), pp. 352–367.*

This research explored whether the reading process would be improved by thinking aloud about texts. Children aged 11–12 were given two versions of a history text and asked to read silently or think aloud about the texts. Children understood and remembered texts better when they thought aloud as they read.

4. *Oster, L (2001) Using the think-aloud for reading instruction,* **The Reading Teacher,** *55 (1), pp. 64–69.*

The think-aloud strategy is described with an explanation of how to introduce it to children. Examples are shown of how the strategy increased the level of child participation as well as their reading and comprehension skills.

Strategy 3: Using key words

Introducing key vocabulary within subject teaching is well established as a strategy for supporting literacy in many secondary schools. In one survey of strategies used by subject teachers to support literacy, 89 per cent of the respondents claimed to use key words with their children (Lewis and Wray, 1999). This wide usage may be because this strategy has a subject-specific dimension as well as a literacy dimension. Focusing on subject-specific vocabulary is an obvious way in which literacy support can be contextualised and both subject teachers and children will recognise the benefits. The learning of key vocabulary can obviously enhance children's subject knowledge but is clearly also helping with their literacy. Introducing 'key words' may offer an immediate and relatively simple way into teaching literacy for teachers who have no training in literacy.

Although an approach through key vocabulary is widely used in secondary classrooms, there are some question marks over how this is done and what the actual benefits are. These benefits may be less than they could be if all that subject teachers do is identify and display key words. There are many other ways of using these key words more interactively, and these strategies can equally be used with primary children.

Firstly, what do we mean exactly by 'key words'? Most obviously, it might consist of words specific to a particular subject. The schemes of work published by QCA are notable for the inclusion of key vocabulary as learning targets for each unit of each subject. For example, for History Unit 1 ('How are our toys different from those in the past?'), QCA suggests that through its study children should be able to understand, use and spell correctly words such as *modern, new, old, before* and *after*. And in Science Unit 5F ('Changing sounds'), the key words specified include *pitch, loudness, vibration, muffle* and *tuning*.

There are a number of ways to focus children's attention on key subject words.

1. Subject-specific dictionaries

Several publishers now produce inexpensive subject-specific dictionaries. These are useful in that children can locate words within them more quickly than in a large, general dictionary. The definitions also give the technical definition first rather than children having to seek it out among several everyday meanings. When a new key word arises, get a child to look up the word in the dictionary and read out the definitions. Discuss and clarify the meanings and get children to define the word in their own words. Encourage the use of these dictionaries on a regular basis.

2. Creating word banks

After an initial brainstorming activity about a subject topic which is about to be studied, the key words arising can be identified and written on pieces of card by children. These cards can then be sorted and displayed alphabetically around the room. New key words might be added at the end of each lesson, having first been identified and defined within the context of the lesson. Constantly revisiting the lists in this way reminds children of their extent and purpose. They should also have their attention drawn to the lists whenever they are undertaking written work. Children could also create their own word lists in the back of their workbooks or highlight the words in their subject dictionaries, if they have a personal copy.

3. Word and definition cards

In some classrooms, teachers have prepared boxes of cards for specific units of work. One set of cards contains the words; another definitions. These can be used for quick matching activities. If the words and their definitions are stored as computer files, children can cut and paste their own prompt sheets using words particularly relevant to them.

4. Key word crosswords/word searches

Children can complete crosswords based on key words and their definitions. Once created, such crosswords can be stored on a computer and become a permanent resource for the school. The crosswords can be of the conventional type with the key word definitions given as clues and the key words being filled in on the crossword grid. Alternatively, children can be given a completed crossword grid and asked to create the clues for each word. Each activity helps reinforce meaning as well as spelling.

5. Creating word clusters

Draw children's attention to the patterns to be found in words (e.g. *equal, equalise, equate, equilateral, equality, equation, equidistant, equilibrium* and so on), pointing out their common root (*equa/equi*, from the Latin word meaning 'to make even') and how that helps with both spelling and meaning. Children can create word cluster posters and display them in subject rooms.

6. Creating mnemonics

Mnemonics are sentences created to help us remember how to spell words or a sequence of facts. The first letter of each word in the sentence is significant. Well known examples include 'Richard of York gave battle in vain' (r, o, y, g, b, i, v – the colours of the rainbow) or 'Big elephants can always use small exits' (because). For homework, children can create a mnemonic to remind them how to spell a key word. The results are shared and one is selected by the class to become their mnemonic of choice. This is written up, displayed and its use encouraged. Children can often come up with very amusing ideas for mnemonic sentences. School mnemonics used by all staff and children for commonly misspelt words can be adopted. For example, to remember how many Ss and Cs are needed in the word 'necessary', the whole school could adopt the sentence, 'It is necessary for a shirt to have one collar and two sleeves'.

7. Creating calligram posters

Calligrams are visual representations of a word that reflect its meaning. For example the word 'test-tube' might be written with an exaggerated letter u which takes on the shape of a test tube:

test tUbe

or 'glacier' might be written in jagged, 'ice letters':

glacier

Again children can create such visual representations of key words and display them for all to share.

8. Creating interactive glossaries

A list of key words from each unit of work is drawn up and written into a small, folded A4 booklet with the words listed alphabetically down the left-hand side of the page and with a blank line alongside each word. A separate sheet of definitions is produced but these are jumbled up and do not match the order of the words in the booklet. Children are given a unit 'glossary', which contains the words but no definitions, to paste into the front of their workbooks. In each lesson two or three key words are stressed (some will be new words, some will be repeats from previous lessons) and used in context. In the last five minutes of the lesson the children find those key words in their glossary booklet. They then find the appropriate definition from the definitions sheet and use this to complete their own glossary by writing in the definitions next to the word. Thus key words are introduced in context and their meaning continuously revisited and revised.

9. Playing word games

The final few minutes of a lesson can profitably be given over to word games that use key vocabulary. There are many such games, including the following examples.

- **Key words can be written at random on an overhead projector (OHP) and projected onto a wall. For example, in maths words such as *quadrilateral, rectangle, square* and so on. When the teacher reads out a definition, two opposing team members compete to be the first to identify and touch the correct word.**
- **Half a word can be written on the OHP and members of opposing teams volunteer to complete the word.**
- **The traditional game of 'hangman' can be played on an OHP using key words.**
- **Everyday terms such as *times* and *share* are written by the teacher and volunteer team members add the 'posh' versions – *multiply, divide* and so on.**
- **You provide the definitions and children write the words.**

Games such as these require little in the way of preparation, can end a session on an upbeat note and help revisit and revise key words in an active and engaging way.

Strategy 4: Visual representation of text

There is an old saying that a picture is worth a thousand words. When it comes to comprehension, this might be paraphrased as: a visual display helps readers understand, organise, and remember some of those thousand words. And the activity of producing a diagrammatic version of the content of a text can be a very powerful aid to comprehension of that text. As an example of this with quite young children, look at the diagram in Figure 4.3. This was produced by 5-year-old Joanne, after having been read an account of the life cycle of a duck. It is clear from the diagram that, although the text was probably too difficult for her to read for herself, she has clearly understood the main points of it and is able to represent these diagrammatically.

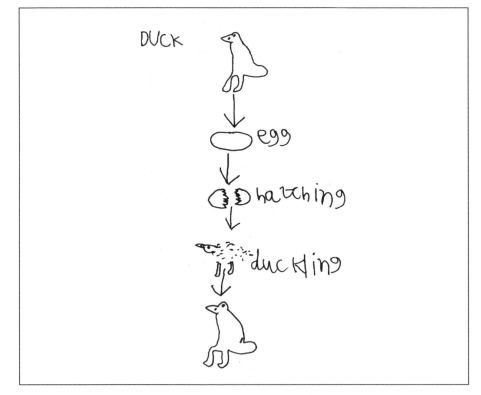

Figure 4.3 *Joanne's life cycle of a duck*

Such reworkings of text content do not need to involve pictorial representations. They can also involve the use of a variety of grid and tabular representations. As an example, look at the grid in Figure 4.4, which was produced by 9-year-old Rachel after some fairly extensive reading about home life in Ancient Greek times. Rachel's teacher had provided her with the grid headings and Rachel's task was to consult a number of books to find out information about the jobs done in the Ancient Greek household, the evidence we have about these jobs and who did them.

Work in the Home

Jobs done in the Home	Evidence Found	who did the work
Cooking	Statue	A woman maybe a Slave
washing	Carving	A Slave or a woman
Sowing and mending	carving	A Woman maybe a Slave
get water	Picture	A woman or a slave
grilling meat	carving	A Slave or a Woman
Careing For children	Picture on a vars	A slave careing for children

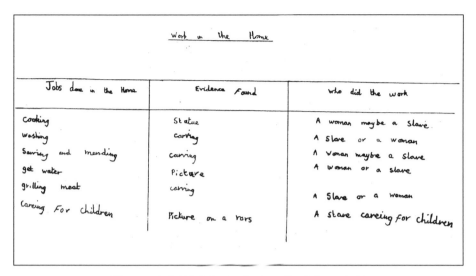

Figure 4.4 *Work in the Ancient Greek household*

It is clear from the grid that most household jobs seemed to fall to a limited number of people in Ancient Greece, and Rachel went on to comment on this fact when she wrote up what she had learnt from this exercise (see Figure 4.5).

working in the home

I found out that ladys do most of the work.

I found out that men are really lazy because they did nothing. but sit around. There is no evidence of working in the house.

There was evidence of washing, cooking carrying, water, grilling meat and caring for children.

The ~~ebit~~ evidence was carvings, statues and paintings.

Rachel

Figure 4.5 *Rachel's comments on the Ancient Greek household*

Research suggests both that presenting children with such visual representations alongside their reading of texts, and asking them to devise their own representations after reading a text, can have a beneficial effect on their understanding.

Practical task

Visual representations

Experiment in the classroom by asking children to represent in a diagrammatic way the content of what they have been reading. There are a couple of ways you might do this:

1. *Use linear, explanation-type texts with the children. Suitable texts might include descriptions of the rain cycle, or of the life cycle of a frog, etc. Ask the children to represent the information in these texts in an arrowed diagram (use Figure 4.2 as a model).*

2. *Use classification-type texts with children. In history, you might find, for example, texts in which you are given information to support both sides of a debate, e.g. 'Was Henry VIII a good king or not?' In science, the questions might be of the type, 'Should we cut trees down, or leave them to grow?'*

Strategy 5: Summarising text

Teaching children to summarise what they read is another way to improve their overall understanding of text. Summarising information requires readers to sift through large units of text, differentiate important from unimportant ideas, and then to synthesise those ideas and create a new coherent text that stands for the original. This sounds difficult, and research demonstrates that, in fact, it is. Most people agree that summarising is a difficult task for many children. Many require teaching of and practice in summarising before they are able to produce good oral and written summaries of text. Research (e.g. National Institute of Child Health and Human Development, 2000) also suggests that teaching children to summarise improves not only their ability to summarise text, but also their overall comprehension of text content.

One way of teaching summarising is to get children to follow a set of steps. For example, they might be taught the following.

1. Rule 1: Delete unnecessary material.

2. Rule 2: Delete redundant material.

3. Rule 3: Think of a word to replace a list of items.

4. Rule 4: Select a topic sentence.

5. Rule 5: Invent a topic sentence if one is not available.

The use of these steps can be seen in the following example (Figure 4.6). The left-hand column shows the original text and the right-hand column shows the deletion of unnecessary and redundant material.

Why do we breathe?	Why do we breathe?
Our bodies are made up of cells, each of which has a special job to do that keeps us alive. Every cell in the body needs oxygen, which allows the cell to get energy brought from the food we eat. Oxygen in the air is brought into the lungs by breathing. The blood collects it from the lungs and takes it to the cells.	~~Our~~ bodies ~~are~~ made up of cells, each ~~of which~~ has a special job ~~to do that keeps us alive~~. Every cell ~~in the body~~ needs oxygen, ~~which~~ allows ~~the~~ cell to get energy from ~~the~~ food ~~we eat~~. Oxygen ~~in the air~~ is brought into ~~the~~ lungs by breathing. ~~The~~ blood ~~collects it from the lungs and~~ takes it to ~~the~~ cells.
Another gas, carbon dioxide, is a waste product of the cells. It is very dangerous if this builds up in the body. The blood carries the carbon dioxide from the cells to the lungs, from where it is breathed out.	~~Another gas~~, carbon dioxide, ~~is a~~ waste product ~~of the cells~~. ~~It is~~ very dangerous if ~~this~~ builds up in ~~the~~ body. ~~The~~ blood carries ~~the~~ carbon dioxide ~~from the cells~~ to the lungs, ~~from where it is~~ breathed out.
When we exercise, our cells are working harder, and they need more oxygen. They also produce more carbon dioxide. That is why we breathe faster when we exercise.	~~When we~~ exercise, ~~our~~ cells ~~are~~ working harder, ~~and they~~ need more oxygen. ~~They also~~ produce more carbon dioxide. ~~That is~~ why we breathe faster ~~when we exercise~~.

Figure 4.6 *Text before and after deleting unnecessary and redundant material*

Figure 4.7 shows the next step in the process: creating topic sentences for each section of the text. In the left-hand column is what remains of the text after the deletion of unnecessary material, and in the right-hand column the topic sentences to summarise each section of this text.

Why do we breathe?	Why do we breathe?
bodies made up of cells, each has special job. Every cell needs oxygen, allows cell to get energy from food. Oxygen brought into lungs by breathing. blood takes it to cells.	Cell needs oxygen and get this by breathing in.
carbon dioxide waste product. Very dangerous if builds up in body. blood carries carbon dioxide to the lungs, breathed out.	Carbon dioxide is breathed out.
exercise, cells work harder, need more oxygen. produce more carbon dioxide. we breathe faster.	When we exercise we need more oxygen and breathe faster.

Figure 4.7 *From text to topic sentences*

Through teacher modelling, group and individual practice, children can learn to apply these rules to create brief summaries of texts they read.

Strategy 6: Questioning

No comprehension activity has a longer tradition than asking children questions about their reading, whether this occurs before, during, or after the reading. We know that children's understanding and recall can be shaped by the types of questions they become accustomed to. Thus if they get a steady diet of factual detail questions, they tend, in future encounters with text, to focus their efforts on factual details. If teachers require more general or more inferential understanding, then they need to emphasise questions that involve that kind of understanding.

An interesting issue about questioning concerns (a) whether children can learn to generate their own questions about text and (b) what impact this might have on their comprehension. The research on this is positive and encouraging. Raphael, for example (Raphael and Pearson, 1985), suggested a technique called QARs (question–answer relationships). This involved teachers modelling and engaging children in differentiating between the types of questions they could ask of text. Children learned to distinguish between three types of questions.

(a) 'Right there' QARs were those where the question and the answer were explicitly stated in the text.
(b) 'Think and search' QARs had questions and answers in the text, but some searching and inferences were required to make the link.
(c) 'On my own' QARs were those in which the question came from the text but the answer had to be generated from the children's prior knowledge.

Research generally suggests that when children learn to generate questions about texts, their comprehension improves.

Strategy 7: Group discussion procedures

There are several activities which involve groups of children problem-solving their ways to reading what are usually 'disrupted' texts. Two of the best known of these activities are cloze and sequencing.

Cloze

Cloze is an activity in which certain words in a passage of text are deleted and the children are asked to complete the text. An example is given in Figure 4.8.

Mount St Helens – an exploding mountain

Mount St Helens is a (——— A ———) in the Rocky Mountain chain of North America. The Rocky (——— B ———) are fold mountains and form part of the North American plate. To the west of the Rockies lies the Pacific plate and the collision zone between the two (——— C ———). The fold mountains were (——— D ———) as a result of sediments being uplifted from the ocean floor as the (——— E ———) and North American plates collided approximately (——— F ———) million years ago.

Figure 4.8 *A sample cloze passage*

This is an activity best used in pairs or groups rather than as a solitary activity, for its value lies in the discussion of possibilities. Completing a cloze text relies upon the readers actively striving to make the text make sense. They may do this in a variety of ways.

- **By using understanding of stylistic features of writing: e.g. at space (A) you could repeat the word *mountain* but would be unlikely to do so as it would mean using it four times in two sentences.**
- **By using the sense of the whole sentence, i.e. the context: at space (B) reading on to the end of the sentence would prompt the missing word.**
- **By drawing upon knowledge of language structures (syntactic knowledge): at point (C) the missing word must be a plural noun as signalled by the use of the article 'the' and the adjective 'two'.**
- **By using existing knowledge: this can be recently acquired, that is, learnt from what you have just read up to that point, as at point (E), or can be information that you simply know or don't know as there is no clue given in the text, as at point (F).**

Having finished the passage by working at completing the meaning a sentence at a time, children should then be encouraged to re-read through the whole piece to check the sense of the whole passage. The pairs/groups should then share their choices with the larger class so alternatives can be aired.

Cloze involves much more than simple guesswork. At best it involves the systematic application of context cues, sensitivity to nuances of meaning and to style, and the articulation of tentative hypotheses about texts. It can also be a very effective way of introducing content knowledge to children. There are a few guiding principles to its use which can help to ensure the maximum benefit.

(i) Choose deletions carefully. The activity seems to work best if words are deleted on the grounds that they are likely to cause discussion. There is little point in deleting words like *the*, *but*, etc., since these generally cause little debate. It is therefore not wise to delete words on a simple numerical basis (for example, every tenth word).

(ii) Leave a lead-in paragraph free from deletions. This may give children the chance to develop some feel for the style of the passage they are working on.

(iii) Have children work on the text in groups of three or four. They may try to complete it individually before discussing their solutions, or complete it as a group straightaway. In either case they should be told to try to achieve an agreed version as this forces them to argue for or against particular suggestions.

(iv) If the children have never used cloze before, they will benefit from working as a group with a teacher. The teacher should not supply correct answers but should rather demonstrate the most useful process of working. Procedures such as listening attentively to another's suggestions, justifying your own ideas, and not being satisfied with the first solution which comes to mind can all be impressed upon the children by the teacher's example.

Sequencing

Like cloze, sequencing can easily be differentiated by careful selection of text and is best undertaken as a collaborative activity which encourages active discussion of meaning. The chosen text is cut up into chunks of several sentences or into individual sentences and the children are asked to reconstruct it into an order which makes sense (which may not be quite the same as the original order – as with cloze, children can often improve upon an author's original text). With younger/less able children it is best to tell them the opening paragraph/sentence but with most children this is not necessary as the game-like conditions of the activity will usually be enough to engage their attention. It is also best to allow children to physically move the text around and try out possibilities.

The text may be split into:

* **paragraphs, which will focus readers' attention onto the flow of meaning within a text;**
* **sentences, which will also concentrate attention on the flow of meaning, but will introduce the importance of linguistic cues, for example, sequence words such as *next*, *afterwards*, or causal words such as *therefore* and *because*;**
* **lines, which will shift attention to predominantly structural cues, especially punctuation and noun/pronoun relationships.**

As an example of a sequencing activity in action, Alexander and Emily were puzzling over a cut-up text about Victorian factories which began with an opening paragraph about the Victorian working day. After trying, and rejecting, one or two pieces to see if they came next Alexander saw a connection.

> Alexander: *Ah! ... Ah! ... this will go there. Look.* (points to a sentence in the opening paragraph). *Look. '16 hours a day'. That would mean working from 6 in the morning to 10 o'clock at night.* (Holds up the next piece he has selected) *'Even for such long hours ...'*

Emily: (nodding) *Yeah, yeah.*
Alexander: *Yeah. That definitely goes there.*

When they had completed the sequencing the whole passage, they were questioned about their choices.

Interviewer: *How did you know that section went there?*
Alexander: *Cos it's still talking about the same thing*
Emily: *It's talking about long hours* (pointing to first paragraph) *then carries on talking about long hours* (pointing to next paragraph).

This kind of textual puzzling, always actively striving for meaning, improves not only the children's use of reading but also their understanding of the subject matter of what they are reading – in this case, history.

Reciprocal teaching

A set of teaching procedures was designed by Palincsar and Brown (1984) to try to develop the reading and comprehension monitoring of a group of children with reading problems. Their approach used what they termed 'reciprocal teaching' to focus upon four activities.

1. Summarising – asking the children to summarise sections of text, thereby encouraging them to focus upon the main ideas in a passage and to check their own understanding of these

2. Questioning – getting the children to ask questions about what they read, again encouraging them to attend to the principal Ideas and to think about their own comprehension of these

3. Clarifying – asking the children to clarify potentially problematic sections of text, requiring them to evaluate the current state of their understanding

4. Predicting – getting them to go beyond the words of the text to make inferences which they must justify by reference to what they read.

Each of these activities had a cognitive and a metacognitive dimension in that not only were the children working upon their comprehension of the texts (comprehension fostering), but they were also having to reflect upon the extent of their comprehension (comprehension monitoring).

The reciprocal teaching procedure involved an interactive 'game' between the teacher and the learners in which each took it in turns to lead a dialogue about a particular section of text. The 'teacher' for each section firstly asked a question, then summarised, then clarified and predicted as appropriate. The real teacher modelled each of these activities and the role played by the children was gradually expanded as time went on from mostly child to mostly teacher.

This procedure was tested on a group of children with reading difficulties. These children did initially experience some difficulties in taking over the role of teacher and needed a lot of help in verbalising during summarising, questioning, clarifying and predicting. Eventually, however, they did become much more accomplished leaders of the comprehension dialogues and showed a very significant improvement on tests of reading comprehension, an improvement which seemed to generalise to other classroom activities and did not fade away after the completion of the research project. Palincsar and Brown attribute the success of their teaching programme to the reciprocal teaching procedure, suggesting that it involved extensive modelling of comprehension fostering and monitoring strategies which are usually difficult to detect in expert readers, that it forced children to take part in dialogues about their understanding even if at a non-expert level and that they learnt from this engagement.

Summary

The aim of this chapter has been to suggest a number of strategies for involving children more actively in the process of reading to understand text across the curriculum. All of the strategies discussed can be used with non-fiction and fiction texts, in a range of curriculum subjects. What they have in common is that they will, at the same time, develop children's reading skills and help them understand more completely the content of the curriculum subject they are dealing with.

References and further reading

Baumann, JF, Jones, LA and Seifert-Kessell, N (1993) Using think alouds to enhance children's comprehension monitoring abilities, *The Reading Teacher*, 47 (3), pp. 184–193.

Kucan, L and Beck, IL (1997) Thinking aloud and reading comprehension research: Inquiry, instruction, and social interaction, *Review of Educational Research*, 67 (3), pp. 271–299.

Lewis, M and Wray, D (1999) Secondary teachers' views and actions concerning literacy and literacy teaching, *Educational Review*, 51 (3), pp. 273–281.

Loxterman, JA, Beck, IL and McKeown, MG (1994) The effects of thinking aloud during reading on students' comprehension of more or less coherent text, *Reading Research Quarterly*, 29 (4), pp. 352–367.

National Institute of Child Health and Human Development (2000) *Report of the National Reading Panel. Teaching children to read: An evidence-based assessment of the scientific research literature on reading and its implications for reading instruction* (NIH Publication No. 00-4769). Washington, DC: US Government Printing Office. (Available online at **www.nichd.nih.gov/publications/nrp/smallbook.htm**).

Oster, L (2001) Using the think-aloud for reading instruction, *The Reading Teacher*, 55 (1), pp. 64–69.

Palincsar, AS and Brown, AL (1984) Reciprocal teaching of comprehension-fostering and comprehension-monitoring activities, *Cognition and Instruction*, 1, pp. 117–175.

Raphael, T and Pearson, PD (1985) Increasing students' awareness of sources of information for answering questions, *American Educational Research Journal*, 22, 217–235.

Wray, D and Lewis, M (1997) *Extending literacy: reading and writing Non-fiction in the Primary School*. London: Routledge. This book explores the topic of reading and writing for information in a thorough way and includes descriptions of many useful strategies in addition to those mentioned in the present chapter. In addition it contains lots of examples of children's work arising from the use of these strategies.

Wray, D and Shilvock, K (2003) *Cross-curricular literacy*. London: Letts Educational. This book largely consists of a collection of texts from a range of subject areas, from mathematics to physical education, along with detailed suggestions about how these texts may be used to develop literacy in subject lessons. It is aimed at younger secondary children, but many of the texts and activities contained here will be suitable for primary children as well.

5 TEACHING NON-FICTION WRITING

Chapter objectives:

The aim of this chapter is to introduce you to:
- *how adults learn to write and the implications of this for how children might be taught to write;*
- *some practical strategies for teaching and developing writing across the curriculum.*

Introduction

A useful way of thinking about the kind of teaching that children need if they are to produce effective writing across the curriculum is to examine the ways in which adults learn to write a new kind of text. How are such adults supported in their writing? When adults write, they usually have access to a wide range of types of support. Think, for example, about young workers who are asked for the first time to prepare a quotation for a job. What support would they have in this situation?

1. Clear criteria for success

Before they start, they know what they have to do and why. They have to specify what needs to be done, the materials to be used, the cost and the time it will take. It has to be priced low enough to get the job and high enough to make a profit.

2. Clear purpose and reader

They know why and to whom they are writing. This helps them make decisions about what information to include/exclude and the level of detail required.

3. Known consequences

They know what is going to happen to their writing. They find out how successful they have been because the client accepts or rejects the quote.

4. Access to models

They can see examples of others' attempts at similar tasks. They can see what information is provided and how it is set out.

5. Access to demonstrations

As apprentices they may have worked alongside other experienced trades people doing similar writing tasks. They will have seen the process of preparing and writing a quote.

6. Guidance during writing

An experienced colleague may 'walk them through' the whole process of preparing a written quote for a job. This person would highlight decisions that need to be made and offer advice on how to make them.

7. Access to guides for writing

Proformas may be provided by the employer explicitly stating what information is to be provided and how.

8. Provision of time

They get time to gather the information that they need. They are not expected to work just from memory. They may also be given a deadline for their final product. The ground rules are very clear.

9. Access to help

There is no penalty for going to others for assistance. In fact, this is expected. Suppliers will provide details required and workmates may pass on tips. When a problem arises, the writers go to a person who can provide solutions.

10. Immediate feedback

Through the questions they are asked about their writing, they get feedback about any lack of clarity or information. They discover how well they have communicated.

Supports such as those listed above are available to adults no matter what kind of writing they are expected to produce.

Practical task

Examining your own writing

Think about a writing task that you have recently been involved in. Examples might range from a job application, the planning for a lesson or scheme of work, a letter to parents, a child's end-of-year report, or an essay assignment. To what extent did you draw upon the supports described above? Jot down some notes about your writing under the following headings.

Clear criteria for success

Did you know what you had to do and why?

Clear purpose and reader

Did you know why and to whom you were writing?

Known consequences

Did you know what was going to happen to your writing?

Access to models

Did you have access to examples of others' attempts at similar tasks?

Access to demonstrations

Did you have an opportunity to work alongside other experienced people doing similar writing tasks?

Guidance during writing

Did you get any guidance from a more experienced colleague as you engaged in the writing?

Access to guides for writing

Did you have access to any proformas for the writing you were engaged in?

Provision of time

Did you get time to gather the information that you would need?

Access to help

Did you get any assistance with your writing?

Immediate feedback

Did you get feedback about any lack of clarity in the writing you did?

For our everyday writing such as letters to friends and shopping lists, support is rarely called upon because the tasks are relatively simple. Access to support becomes more important the more complicated or significant the writing and the more inexperienced the writer. It becomes crucial when the writing has really important consequences – such as in a job application.

The implications of teaching

Adults are often faced with new writing challenges. Those who meet these challenges successfully have strategies for identifying and using the range of support available to them. Even the most experienced writers call on this support from time to time. The question is, can teachers give children in classrooms the same support that is available to adults?

Classroom research suggests that they can. As well as making writing tasks relevant, purposeful and satisfying, they can make explicit for children how written texts work, and how writers operate when writing particular texts.

In the rest of this chapter I will explore some of the strategies that teachers can use to do this, including:

1. providing models of writing and focusing children's attention on how these work;

2. demonstrating writing processes;

3. participating in writing tasks alongside children;

4. scaffolding children in producing writing.

1. Providing and studying models of written work

'Show me some examples!' is a familiar request from people who are trying to learn new things. When learners are provided with examples, or models, of the kinds of written work they are asked to create, this offers them an opportunity to identify the distinctive features of the product. Often if children are asked to explain how they tell the difference between one type of writing and another, they show very little explicit awareness of the distinguishing features. Using models can help children identify the characteristics of types of writing and enable them to set specific goals for improving their writing or for monitoring and reviewing their efforts in a particular task. Through the examination of models, children get to see what it is that they need to learn to do. This strategy can be particularly valuable when they are asked to produce a type or style of writing that is unfamiliar to them, such as a business letter, a science report, a 'spooky' story or a compare-and-contrast essay.

There are a number of issues to consider when using models with children. The following guidelines will be useful when planning work with models so that children can apply what they learn to their own writing.

Models should be provided when children most need them
The best times to provide models are before children need to do a similar kind of writing themselves, or when they are having difficulties in their own writing. They are then able to see the activity as relevant to their learning needs. They will have an immediate opportunity to try some of the features of the models in their own writing.

Models should be complete texts

Children will benefit from seeing complete texts rather than extracts, so that they can discern overall structural, organisational and formatting features. Where the focus is for the children to consider specific features of writing, such as the mechanics, it may be appropriate to provide copies of extracts after the entire text has been read aloud.

Models should be read aloud to children

If the teacher reads model texts aloud, this gives children the chance to familiarise themselves with the meanings of the text without having to do the hard, and distracting, work of decoding these texts for themselves. When they subsequently analyse the texts, the fact that they already know what they mean will be a major benefit since it allows them to concentrate upon the job at hand.

Children need several models

Limiting analysis to just one text example does not allow children to decide which features of the model being used are critical. To take a very simple example, if children were presented with only one model of a newspaper birth announcement that happened to be written in a style that suggested the baby was 'writing', e.g. *Hi, I'm Kylie Emma Smith and I was born on . . .*, the children would have no way of knowing whether or not such a writing style was a critical characteristic of that form of writing. Presenting a range of birth announcements allows children to see that some features are critical, i.e. name, date of birth, parents' names, etc., whereas others, such as the style of writing, are not.

Looking at several models of the same kind of writing will also build children's awareness of the options and alternatives that writers have available to them. In addition, it encourages children to view models as a resource they can use rather than as an ideal they must imitate.

Children should have individual copies of models

If the children have individual copies of each model, they are free to mark the text as necessary. For example, they might highlight main idea statements in one colour and supporting details in another. Alternatively, they may label parts of the text or write notes in the margin.

Children should be asked to develop lists of the features of a text

It is better to ask children to generate their own lists of features that describe how the models of writing work. Telling them exactly what they should find tends to constrain their thinking and prevents them from drawing on their combined knowledge of how texts work. Finding out which features children automatically identify is also a useful way for the teacher to learn about their current understandings of, and strategies for, analysing and thinking about written texts. Children can, however, be invited to focus on general features, for example, 'How have the writers structured their texts?' or 'How have they created a particular mood or atmosphere?' or 'How have they set out their letters?'

As an example of this process, Miss R's Year 5 class was beginning some work on writing instructional texts. She began by using as a model text a recipe for making pizza. After reading the text together, the class discussed the following points (the key points which the teacher was trying to draw out are given in italics).

- **How do you know this is a recipe?** (*It tells you how to cook something. There's a list of ingredients.*)
- **What kind of text is that?** (*It tells you how to do something. Instructions.*)
- **Can you think of any other texts that are like recipes and tell you how to do something?** (*Rules for playing games. Instructions for fixing the computer.*)
- **What does a recipe always begin with?** (*There will always be a title. The title tells you what you are going to make.*)
- **What does the first part of this recipe tell you?** (*How big a pizza it will make. How long it takes.*)
- **What does the next part tell you?** (*The ingredients. What you need to make the pizza.*)
- **How are the ingredients organised?** (*A list. Measurements for each item.*)
- **What follows the ingredients?** (*What you have to do. The method.*)
- **What do you notice about these directions?** (*They are often in the form of a numbered list. They use commands, or imperatives. They refer to time, either directly or by the use of chronological connectives – until, then, etc.*)

Miss R then went on to ask her children to compile a checklist of the crucial features of a recipe. This was a useful learning activity in its own right as it forced the children to think abstractly about text features. It was also used later as an aide-mémoire when they came to write their own recipes. The questions Miss R used to prompt the children, together with some of the points she hoped they would notice and some of the answers they actually gave, are given in Figure 5.1.

Thinking about recipes		
Questions the children were asked	**Teaching points**	**Some of the children's responses**
What comes first in a recipe?	The title of the dish. The goal of the recipe	What you're going to make. The name of what you're making
What comes next?	List of ingredients	What you need. All your equipment and things
How are these laid out on the page?	Vertical list flushed left	A list

▶

In what order are the ingredients listed?	This is debatable	The order in which you use them. The biggest things first
What comes next in the recipe?	Directions for making the dish	What you have to do
In what order are these listed?	Chronological .	The right order
Why?	Because that's how you use them	You'd get mixed up
How are they laid out on the page?	Usually a numbered list	Number of steps. 1, 2, 3, 4 ...
What tense are they written in?	Imperative	Do this ...
Do they use passive or active verbs?	Active	You have to do actions
Who is the audience for a recipe?	There is an implied second person – an implied but not stated 'you'	Anyone making the dish. The cook
What style of language would you expect?	Unembellished, businesslike, formal	Plain and simple
Why?	Ease of use – you need instant reference	It has to be quick to read

Figure 5.1 *Analysing a recipe*

Children should work in groups

The most effective way for children to work in activities like this is when they collaborate in small groups or pairs. After they have been working in groups they can then be brought together for a report-back session with the whole class. Enlarged copies of the models on large sheets of paper or overhead projector transparencies can be useful when discussing and summarising group findings.

Children can help develop writing guides

An effective way of helping children make the connection between analysing models and their own writing is to develop writing guides with them. These guides remind children of the features they need to think about when they write. They can be displayed on a chart in the classroom or duplicated for children to use as they write. An example of a writing guide to help children structure their persuasive writing is given in Figure 5.2 below.

What will your persuasive writing be about?	
Who is the audience?	
What will be the aim of your writing?	
What illustrations will you use?	
What layout will you use?	
What kind of sentences will you mostly use?	
List some of the words you might use	
Alliteration	Exaggeration
Persuasive	Rhyming

Figure 5.2 *A writing guide for persuasive writing*

Other writing guides might be developed with children to identify features such as how writers create a particular atmosphere and mood, or develop characters in their work. These may take the form of lists of words and phrases children can use when they write, or a list of the characteristics that children need to include when they describe a character.

Writing guides can help children.

- **They remove some of the decisions they have to make as they write, providing a frame for them to plan and think about their writing as a whole;**
- **They help them to set specific goals to achieve in a writing task. Children can refer to the guide and ask themselves, 'Does my writing have the features listed on the guide?'**
- **They help them to solve writing problems independently. Children can often find the help they need by referring to a guide instead of asking the teacher.**
- **They allow them to provide specific help for each other. When children find it difficult to incorporate a particular feature on a guide into their writing they have, in effect, identified a writing problem and can seek specific help for solving it from their peers.**

Guides also become a useful tool for discussing children's writing with them. One teacher described how she used the features lists developed by her children to guide her discussions with them about their writing.

> When I looked at the children's writing I used a photocopy of the features list we devised as a checklist to give them feedback. If an aspect on the list was included by a child, I ticked the box. If there were omissions which should have been included, I put a question mark. However, if the omission was allowable I put a dash in the box. I found this an extraordinarily simple way of providing feedback.

Developing writing guides with children gives them support to be successful in their writing. Children can use them as a resource rather than as recipes that must be slavishly followed. If they have access to several organisational or structural guides for particular types of writing, they can select the form that best suits their ideas, purposes and audience.

2. Demonstrating writing processes

'Show me how!' is another familiar request from people learning something new. A demonstration by a proficient person offers learners insights into how they might do something themselves. But, unlike many practical activities in the trades and the arts, the tools of the writer's craft are predominantly held in the head, not the hand. Consequently, much of what proficient writers do is not immediately accessible to learners. Although observers can see writers move the pen, pause and make changes to what has been written, the actual decisions they make and the way they make them remains hidden. As a result, people often believe that writing just happens – magically flowing from writers' minds onto the page. As one Year 3 child said, 'Writing is easy. You just get ideas in your head, then they come down into your shoulder and along your arm and on to the page.' Indeed, if children are asked what they think makes a good writer, they may reveal misconceptions such as the following:

- **that the easier the writing flows onto the page, the better writer you are;**
- **that the work of writing is almost finished once the first draft is done;**
- **that once a draft is done all that is required is to correct conventional errors such as spelling and punctuation.**

Children can be helped by the teacher demonstrating how he/she operates as a writer. This shared writing can be done by the teacher writing in front of children on large sheets of paper or an overhead projector so that they can see the writing in progress. As the adult writes, he/she 'thinks aloud', giving children a running commentary on the thinking needed in order to write.

This is an ideal way of making the hidden thinking processes of writing explicit for learners. From these demonstrations children will be able to see that writing requires constant decision-making. They will see the adult confront problems about such things as topic, readership, ideas, organisation, language and conventions. They will also see how the adult manages this complex task by dealing, as much as possible, with one problem at a time. They will see him/her:

- **selecting or clarifying the writing task;**
- **collecting and connecting information;**
- **gathering ideas and researching;**
- **planning;**
- **writing, reading and revising;**
- **doing final editing and proofreading;**
- **getting feedback.**

What makes demonstration such a rich experience for children is the opportunity it provides for them to see the process of writing – not just the product of it. Children actually see why particular features of writing, such as spelling and grammar, are important to writers as well as when it is most appropriate to deal with them and how they can be dealt with. During a demonstration the pressure is off for children. They can focus on whatever is relevant to their writing needs.

Demonstrations can be given of any type of writing. Children are likely to appreciate seeing how an experienced writer tackles the kinds of tasks they are asked to do such as science reports, stories or history essays, especially if these are new or unfamiliar to them. Children can also learn a great deal by watching the adult work on writing tasks done for purposes beyond the classroom – that letter to the bank manager, or to parents or the editor of a newspaper. Children are often very interested in finding out what their teachers do when they write and they will try to use the strategies they have been shown in their own writing.

Demonstrations do not have to be time consuming or complicated. Because they are intense observation activities it is probably best not to spend more than 10 or 15 minutes at a time demonstrating. A short demonstration can be a routine feature of lessons or run a more intense series over a short period of time.

Sometimes, there may not be time in class to demonstrate the entire process of writing one text from beginning to end. Instead, what teachers can do is to demonstrate various stages in the process, doing some of the writing away from the children. This writing can then be shown to the children, with a brief explanation of how that stage in the task was reached and time allowed for them to ask questions about it before the teacher goes on to demonstrate the next stage. For example, the teacher might demonstrate using a cut-and-paste strategy or ways of tackling planning of the text. There may also be a focus on features of written products that are causing children difficulty, such as writing an effective conclusion to an essay or using quotation marks accurately.

To help children make the connection between demonstrations and their independent writing, it can be useful to develop process guides with them. Like the writing guides described earlier, process guides remind children of the problem-solving strategies they can apply while they are writing. These guides can also take the form of wall charts or duplicated sheets for children to use as they write. Typically, process guides are reminders of the sorts of questions successful writers ask themselves as they write, or as they re-read their writing in preparation for a second draft. For example, one teacher provided his Year 6 children with the process guide shown in Figure 5.3 below. The children used this guide to self-monitor their writing processes before, during and after writing and as a discussion starter when they shared their writing with each other.

Before writing	Why do I want to write about this topic?
	How will I develop my ideas?
	Who will I discuss it with?
	My initial plan is ...
	Who will read this piece?
	What do I want it to do to/for them?
During writing	Am I thinking about my reader by including:
	excitement, humour, suspense, my opinions?
	Am I thinking about how this will end?
	Will it help if I check out what I have written with someone else?
After writing	Have my readers responded as I hoped?
	Can I change the language to make it more effective?
	What words are there that I have not used before in my writing?
	My favourite sentence is ...
	Have I read the entire piece aloud to myself and to one other person?
	Have I underlined words I think I may have misspelled?
	Have I checked full stops, capitals and speech marks?

Figure 5.3 *A writing process checklist*

3. Participating in writing tasks alongside children

'Do it with me!' is yet another request likely to be heard when new things are shown and demonstrated to people. Novice writers often find it difficult to integrate effectively all they must think about and do as they write. As a result, they can easily get stuck in writing ruts, focusing too much of their attention on the wrong issues at the wrong time. For example, children may give too much of their early attention to solving spelling problems, or they may focus too much on text structure before they have worked out what ideas and information they have to write about. The surprising thing is that, even when children can talk sensibly about effective writing processes and product features, they may not be able to translate this easily into practice in their own writing. If the teacher participates with children as they attempt a new or difficult writing task, this can help them make the transition from knowing about writing processes and text features to actually being able to use this knowledge in their own writing.

When teachers participate with children in completing a writing task, the best role they can take is a guiding, supportive one. For example, they may take responsibility for scribing the text and guiding its production although it is the children who are actually doing the composing. In this way both teacher and children participate in creating the written text and completing a task that the children may not normally be able to do successfully on their own. The idea is for the teacher to set up children to think and make writing decisions in collaboration with their peers, possibly with the occasional suggestion from above. This is what distinguishes this approach from process demonstrations where teachers show children how they make writing decisions. Through the questions posed and the input offered to the group, teachers can frame and guide children's thinking by making writing problems explicit, and challenge children to solve them.

Writing with children can, at times, be successful with large groups or even the whole class, but it probably operates best with a small group of about five children. This allows all members of the group to actively negotiate the making of the text – the central purpose of the activity.

Since teachers can usually write faster than any of the children, a useful role is to act as scribe. This frees the children to keep thinking while someone else does the physical writing. If this writing is done on large sheets of paper then everyone will be able to see it clearly and re-read whenever they need to. The kinds of questions the teacher asks and the input he/she offers during a participatory writing activity are the keys to its success. For example, teachers can do the following.

- **Ensure that the topic is one where the children share some knowledge or experience.**
- **Make sure children are clear about the purpose of and likely readers for the writing task from the beginning by asking, 'What's our writing task? Why are we doing it? Who is going to read it? What do we need to tell our readers? What type of writing do you think will suit our purposes?'**
- **Activate children's existing knowledge by recalling other occasions when they have written for similar purposes and readers, or by reviewing demonstrations, models and guides that they have seen and used.**
- **Get children to brainstorm ideas and information for writing by asking, 'What do you know about the topic?' If necessary this can lead to further research to gather more information.**
- **Help children think about ways of organising their 'brainstorm' list as a way of planning their writing. 'How can we organise our ideas? Can you group any together into categories? How will we begin our writing (report/essay/story, etc.)?'**
- **Help children draw on their existing knowledge and experience to solve writing problems that come up. 'Remember when we ... ? Can you do something similar here?'**
- **Show children how to use writing and process guides that they have developed in earlier activities as a resource for solving problems they encounter in their writing. 'Look back at ... Is that guide any help to us now?'**

- Frequently re-read the developing text to the group to encourage children to monitor meaning and plan ahead before composing more text. 'How does what we've just written fit with our introduction?' or 'What do we need to include next?' Sometimes it may be necessary to go right back to the beginning of the text; at other times re-reading only a few sentences will do when children are stuck.

- Suggest solutions to problems from which they can choose the option they think is most appropriate. 'Some things you could do here are ... Which one do you think would work best?'

- Show children how different solutions might work in their writing. For example, teachers might try out different beginnings on scrap paper, reorganise an intro-duction so children can compare it with the original version, model alternative ways of expressing the same meaning, etc.

- Take on the role of the reader for the children by pointing out any inconsisten-cies or vague meanings. 'If I were another child reading this I don't think I would understand what you mean by ... Can you make it clearer?' or 'Can you expand on this point?' Teachers might also respond positively when the group has done something well. 'That makes it very clear, I know exactly what you mean there.'

- Allow children to 'think aloud' as they make suggestions to the group and help them to translate this into effective written language. 'Is that what you mean ...? How could you write that down so your readers understand?'

- Help children to clarify their understanding of the content or ideas they are writing about. Sometimes children will reveal that their difficulties in solving a problem are not due to lack of writing ability but more to do with confused concepts or misinterpreted information.

- Involve children in making decisions about how the writing will be published and presented to intended readers and about how they will get a response to their work.

Teachers have a dual role when they participate in writing tasks with children. They are there not only to guide children through the process of writing but also to work at developing their group co-operation and discussion skills. Helping them to estab-lish an effective pattern of interaction and collaboration on tasks with their peers can offer a model for working effectively in groups when the teacher is not present.

Children will engage more enthusiastically in a participatory writing activity when the writing task they are working on serves a clear purpose. The group may, for example, be working to research part of a topic being explored by the whole class. Their task for participatory writing could be that of writing a report of their research findings for other children in the class to read and learn from. Alternatively, a group may work with the teacher to produce a model essay for other children to respond to and discuss. Whatever the purpose, as long as children believe the task is likely to have satisfying consequences for them, they will probably try hard to do it well.

In collaboration it can be difficult for the teacher not to make writing decisions for the children – especially when they suggest things which seem inappropriate. However, if teachers write or change the text without consulting the children who were responsible for it, this will lessen the learning opportunities for the children. The idea is for the children to participate in the decision-making so that they can operate more effectively on their own later. What the teacher can do is alert them to any inappropriate decisions they may make, by discussing an alternative point of view from a reader of the text. If, despite the advice of the teacher, the children do not choose the most appropriate option, this should be allowed to stand. In this way children can be shown that their viewpoints are taken seriously.

The teacher's role in participatory writing is to foster children's decision-making processes during writing. This can be a powerful strategy for helping children develop their knowledge of writing and writing processes.

4. Scaffolding children in producing writing

'Help me do it!' is also something that learners of a process often say as they take their first faltering steps. Think of babies who have witnessed countless people walking and are desperate to master this process for themselves; or young children who have seen older siblings ride their bicycles and want to copy; or children who have seen others swimming and want to do the same. In none of these cases can the learner simply move in one bound from observing demonstrations to performing the action completely independently. They need support – adult hands holding them up, allowing them to perform the action, and gradually, over some time, withdrawing until independence is achieved. Learning to write is no different from these other actions – it needs the support of more accomplished practitioners to enable learners to be successful even in their early attempts. Some children will learn most of what they need to know about writing a particular kind of text from the demonstrations of writing they have experienced. For many, however, the jump from being shown how to write in a particular way to being able to write that way independently is simply too big for them to make easily. They need more support as they begin to learn to be independent writers.

This phase involves scaffolded writing, during which teachers can offer children strategies to aid their writing, which they can use without an adult necessarily being alongside them. One such strategy is the use of writing frames, which can act both as a way of increasing a child's experience of a particular type of writing and as a substitute for the teacher's direct interventions which encourage children to extend their writing.

A writing frame consists of a skeleton outline to scaffold children's writing of a particular text type. The skeleton framework consists of different key words or phrases, according to the particular generic form. The template of starters, connectives and sentence modifiers which constitute a writing frame gives children a structure within which they can concentrate on communicating what they want to say, rather than getting lost in the form. However, by using the form, children become increasingly familiar with it.

An example writing frame for scaffolding persuasive writing is given in Figure 5.4.

Although not everybody would agree, I want to argue that
I have several reasons for arguing for this point of view. My first reason is
A further reason is
Furthermore
Therefore, although some people argue that
I think I have shown that

Figure 5.4 *A persuasive writing frame*

One example of a child's use of this frame is given below in Figure 5.5.

Although some people would not agree I want to argue that too many people are making a noise as they pass our classroom. There is also a lot of noise when people mess about and shout in the toilets.

I have quite a few reasons for arguing this. Firstly, when I am trying to work people make noise outside and I can't concentrate.

Another reason is that when I am talking to my teacher or to other children people make noise outside and we have to speak louder and then our class gets noisy or if she is reading us a story we might not be able to hear her.

So even though some people might say they don't care or that it isn't them, I think I have shown that everyone needs to be quieter, as quiet as mice.

Figure 5.5 *Scaffolded persuasive writing*

An example writing frame for recount writing is given in Figure 5.6.

Before I began this topic I thought that
But when I read about it I found out that
I also learnt that
Furthermore I learnt that
Finally I learnt that

Figure 5.6 *A recount writing frame*

One example of a child's use of this frame is given in Figure 5.7.

Before I began this topic I thought that the male rabbits where the ones who dug the warrens. But when I read about it I found out that it was actual the females who did all the work, as usual!
I also learnt that the passages or burrows are up to 3m long and 15 cm wide so the rabbits can get though easily.
Secondly I learnt that the warren can be over 80 years old and around 30 rabbits can live in one.
Finally I learnt that the rabbits warren has lots of ways in and out, so if one is blocked a rabbit can get in another. Also a warren is only for one family.

Figure 5.7 *A scaffolded recount*

Notice how writing with this kind of frame scaffolds writing in a number of ways.

- **It does not present writers with a blank page. There is comfort in the fact that there is already some writing on this page. This alone can be enough to encourage weaker writers to write at greater length.**
- **The frame provides a series of prompts to children's writing. Using the frame is rather like having a dialogue with the page, and the prompts serve to model the register of that particular piece of writing.**
- **The frame deliberately includes connectives beyond the simple 'and then'. Extended use of frames can result in children spontaneously using these more elaborate connectives in other writing.**
- **The frame is designed around the typical structure of a particular genre. It thus gives children access to this structure and implicitly teaches them a way of writing this type of text.**

The use of a frame should always begin with shared writing, discussion and teacher modelling before moving on to collaborative writing (teacher and children together) and then to the children undertaking writing supported by the frame. This oral, teacher modelling, joint construction pattern of teaching is vital for it not only models the generic form and teaches the words that signal connections and transitions but it also provides opportunities for developing children's oral language and their thinking. Some children, especially those with learning difficulties, may need many oral sessions and sessions in which their teacher acts as a scribe before they are ready to attempt their own writing.

It is useful to make 'big' versions of the frames for use in shared writing. It is important that the children understand that the frame is a supportive draft and words may be crossed out or substituted. Extra sentences may be added or surplus starters crossed out. The frame should be treated as a flexible aid, not a rigid form.

When the children have a purpose for writing they may be offered a frame:
- **When they first attempt independent writing in an unfamiliar text type and a scaffold might be helpful to them.**
- **When they appear stuck in a particular mode of writing, e.g. constantly using 'and then ... and then' when writing an account.**
- **When they 'wander' between text types in a way that demonstrates a lack of understanding of a particular type, e.g. while writing an instructional text such as a recipe they start in the second person (*First you beat the egg*) but then shift into a recount (*Next I stirred in the flour*).**
- **When they have written something in one structure (often a personal recount) which would be more appropriate in a different form, e.g. writing up a science experiment as a personal recount.**

Writing frames can be helpful to children of all ages and all abilities. They are particularly useful, however, with children of average writing ability and with those who find writing difficult. It would of course be unnecessary to use the frame with writers already confident and fluent in a particular text type but they can be used to introduce such writers to new types. The aim with all children is for them to reach the stage of assimilating the generic structures and language features into their independent writing repertoires. Children, therefore, need to use the frames less and less as their knowledge of a particular form increases. At this later stage, when children begin to show evidence of independent usage, they may need only to have a master copy of the frames available as help cards for those occasions when they need a prompt. A box of such help cards could be a part of the writing area in which children are encouraged to refer to many different aids to their writing. This is one way of encouraging children to begin to make independent decisions about their own learning.

Summary

In this chapter we have made a close examination of the various processes involved in the production of writing for whatever purpose. I have described a number of generic strategies for introducing these strategies to children. It is important to think about such strategies as part of a larger whole. Many teachers, for example, are so impressed with the usefulness of writing frames that they use them without fitting them into the full process of writing that I have described here. This is a mistake. No single teaching strategy will solve all the writing problems of the children in your class, but the coherent use of a range of strategies may be of great benefit.

References and further reading

Lewis, M and Wray, D (1997) *Writing frames*. Reading: University of Reading Reading and Language Information Centre.

Wray, D and Lewis, M (1998) *Writing across the curriculum*. Reading: University of Reading Reading and Language Information Centre. These two books contain lots of examples of blank writing frames for use with children. In the first book the frames are ordered according to text type, with frames to scaffold recounts, reports, explanations, persuasion, discussion and instructions. In the second book the emphasis is on frames for a variety of subject areas, and here you will find writing frames for use in science, mathematics, technology, and so on.

6 LITERACY ACROSS THE PRIMARY CURRICULUM: LOOKING AT SCIENCE

Chapter objectives:

The aim of this chapter is to introduce you to:
- *the place of literacy within science and the text types which are characteristic of this curriculum subject;*
- *a teaching approach to developing literacy within science.*

Introducing literacy into science

Let us begin with a typical introduction to a science lesson. Mrs Smith is leading a science lesson with her Year 6 class. Their topic for this term is volcanoes.

Teacher:	*Now children, we are going to be looking at volcanoes this term. Did any of you see the film* Dante's Peak *on the television last week?*
Child 1:	*It was great; when it blew up, the whole town was destroyed.*
Child 2:	*I saw a volcano on television in a different programme. It was like this big mountain, we watched and you could see this red runny stuff come out and clouds came off it.*
Teacher:	*Does anyone know what scientists call the red runny stuff?*
Child 2:	*Lava.* (Teacher writes 'lava' on the board.)
Teacher:	*What do we call it when a volcano blows up?*
Child 3:	*Erupts.* (Teacher writes 'erupts' on the board.)
Teacher:	*How do you think a scientist would describe the volcanic explosion?*
Child 4:	*When a volcano erupts, lava flows out …*

In this brief extract we can see that the teacher is providing a scaffold for the children's learning in a number of ways.

- **She activates and makes links with their prior knowledge, which may come from home contexts or from previous school experiences.**
- **She provides them with a visual trigger to activate their responses.**
- **She explicitly teaches subject-specific vocabulary and moves the children from their commonsense understandings of the topic to the technical understandings required in the subject.**

As teachers we need to provide explicit teaching to enable our children to meet the literacy demands of various subject areas. This explicit teaching of literacy is central to the teaching of the subject content.

What is literacy in science?

'Literacy' is a word with a very broad range of meanings. We can talk about scientific literacy, computer literacy, media literacy, and so on. When literacy is used in these ways it generally means something like 'understanding and applying'. So what we really mean is understanding and applying science, understanding and applying computers or understanding the media.

In order to understand and apply science we need not just to understand scientific processes, but to be able to extend our knowledge of these processes and to apply that knowledge to new situations, which sometimes involves providing explanations of this knowledge to other people who are collaborating in the application of the ideas. Understanding and applying science therefore involves reading science texts, reading being the major way we extend our knowledge in most areas of life. (Of course, we also extend knowledge through hands-on experiences, but the amount of scientific material we can actually experience at first hand is quite limited. How did you learn what you know about volcanoes?) Explaining the science we know also involves written texts. The fact is that scientists write – a lot. They write to explain their thoughts about the subjects they are dealing with, sometimes to peers and sometimes to learners.

It is important to assist children with these literacy skills because the systematic and explicit teaching and learning of science content are made more difficult when children are unable to listen, speak, read and write appropriately. For effective learning in science, children need to be able to use literacy skills to analyse and respond to the world around them, to construct knowledge in a systematic way and to convey their understandings to others. In science, children are expected to listen, talk, read and write for such purposes as: describing, classifying, predicting, instructing, summarising, discussing, arguing, explaining and recounting.

Practical task

Literacy in science

Think about the ways in which children might use the four language modes listed above (listening, speaking, reading and writing). Jot down some possible uses of these modes in the learning of this subject.

1. *How might children use listening to learn science?*

2. *How might children use speaking to learn science?*

3. *How might children use reading to learn science?*

4. *How might children use writing to learn science?*

Listening

In science, effective listening allows children to gain information and follow instructions. Children can also analyse speech critically to ascertain the purpose of the speaker, so they can respond appropriately. To do this they need to recognise the structure of language and be able to detect the intention of a speaker. They need to interact in group processes and seek clarification. Effective listeners attend to tone of voice, language used (emotive versus factual, degree of certainty or confidence), body language and the relationship established between the speaker and the listener.

Speaking

Speaking in science assists children to link prior understanding to new knowledge. Speech engages the learner and allows the sharing, reflection and modification of thoughts so that children can better construct scientific meaning. It can also assist children to recognise and pronounce unfamiliar words. Speaking activities in science lessons help prepare children for reading and writing tasks and so it is important for children to be able to choose the forms of speaking appropriate to their purpose, audience and context. By listening to children speaking, teachers can determine their prior understanding and monitor and assess their learning.

Reading

Children need to read in order to expand their view of and interest in the world of science. Additionally, through reading they can expand their understanding of science. In science, children need to read so that they can follow instructions and obtain information. We should be encouraging our children to gather information from a variety of sources, including books, newspapers, magazines, videos, slides, multimedia and the internet. While reading, it is useful for children to recognise the organisational elements in texts. This will assist them to recognise the purposes within text and to critically analyse it to determine whether or how the writer is attempting to influence them. Children studying science also need to recognise that scientific diagrams, tables and graphs, symbols and mathematical relationships can also be used to explain, describe, instruct and argue. When children transform these familiar scientific recording systems into appropriate written texts, they need to refine and express their understandings. They should also be able to transfer written texts into graphic and symbolic representations. Children should be encouraged to use a variety of reading skills including: skimming and scanning techniques; re-reading; consulting indexes, contents, glossaries.

Writing

In science, children are expected to write in order to share their findings and understandings, to clarify meaning, to respond to information presented to them and to present a particular point of view. Science presents a myriad of opportunities to develop a range of literacy skills in writing because science topic knowledge can be built through practical activities in the first instance. Children who are not confident readers can become successful writers through knowledge of how texts are structured. This knowledge will then assist their reading. To be successful in writing in science, children need to be able to apply an understanding of the way different types of texts are organised so that they can construct a text appropriate for their purpose and audience. Children need to recognise that in scientific writing it is especially important to choose appropriate technical words (like *mass, velocity, condensation* and *solution*) and to use numerical relationships, diagrams, tables, graphs, flow charts and drawings to convey meaning. Children should recognise that the process of writing involves planning, gathering and sorting information, drafting, conferencing, proofreading, editing and presenting.

Text types in science

Underpinning all the material in this book is a view that language is produced in response to a range of purposes. All these language productions, whether spoken or written, formal or informal, are called 'texts'. The particular language choices we make in any situation influence, and are influenced by, the people involved, the subject matter and how the message is communicated. The roles and relationships existing between the speaker and the listener or between the reader and the writer influence the words which will be used and the ways in which the text will be structured. The subject matter will also influence the language choices. In a science text for children you would expect to find language which instructs, such as *collect equipment* and *record information in a table*. You would also expect to find words which name the equipment to be used, such as *test tube* and *filter paper*; processes such as *observe, record, conclude*; and technical words which relate to scientific concepts such as *reaction, velocity, mass* and *hypothesis*.

During their primary years children are engaged in talking, listening, reading and writing for a range of purposes which lead them to become familiar with a variety of different forms of reading, writing, talking and listening. These different forms of language are often called 'text types'. We can group them together, based on features they have in common, and, as we did in Chapter 5, give them names, such as: discussion, explanation, instructions, recount, report, persuasion. Children's skills in recognising and using these text types need to be developed not just in their literacy lessons, but also in the contexts where these text types have real purpose, such as in science lessons.

In science, children are likely to be asked to listen to, read, produce orally and write the following text types:

- **reports – texts giving information about a phenomenon, for example, *whales, the food chain in a forest, permeable and impermeable materials*;**
- **sets of instructions – instructions for how to perform a particular scientific procedure, for example, *investigating materials which dissolve in water*;**
- **recounts – texts giving accounts of how scientific processes and investigations were carried out, for example, *our investigations into evaporation of water*;**

- explanations – texts giving reasons for particular scientific phenomena, for example, *the rain cycle*;
- discussions – texts giving arguments for and against particular courses of action, for example, *should we build more nuclear power stations?*
- arguments – texts giving a set of reasons in support of a position or action, for example, *experiments on animals should be banned.*

Practical task

Examining a science activity

Think about a science activity you have taught recently and try to analyse the text types which you asked at least some children in your class to read and/or write. Use a grid like the following to record what you have found.

Text type	Children read texts like this	Children wrote texts like this
Reports		
Instructions		
Recounts		
Explanations		
Discussions		
Arguments		

Were you surprised and/or satisfied with the range of text types involved in this activity? Can you think of any ways in which you might have expanded this range of text types?

While initially children will be examining such text types in isolation, many of the tasks that confront them will require them to incorporate the features of several different text types. Many of the tasks in which children will be involved during subject lessons will require them to incorporate the features of several text types. Consider a task like the following: *Identify ten processed foods which you can buy or which you have at home. Describe the additives in them and discuss the health benefits or risks of these.* Children need to be shown how to break up this task into its component parts. What is this task actually asking of the children?

1. *Identify ten processed foods* requires children to look at a number of food products and read the packaging to determine which have additives. They would then need to locate the information about additives on the packaging, list these, and probably classify them depending upon whether they are, for example, *food colours, preservatives* or *flavour enhancers*. Children might require assistance with finding where on the packaging this information is located and with reading the names and symbols used to describe them. The teacher would probably need to develop the children's understandings of these additives using spoken language, so that they can read them with understanding and reproduce them correctly in writing.

2. *Describe the additives in them* requires children to define processed foods and list some examples with their additives. They might use a table and would probably include an explanation of the purpose of some of the additives.

3. *Discuss the health benefits* requires children to provide information about the benefits of some food additives.

4. *Discuss the health risks* requires children to provide information about the risks of some food additives. Often tasks such as these require children to conclude with a recommendation or a general statement about the benefits and risks.

When setting tasks such as this, it is important that you are clear about the purpose of the task and what you expect the children to produce, and that you explain this clearly. It is particularly important that you make explicit the criteria which will be used to evaluate their outcomes.

The literacy demands of science

The literacy demands of science include:

- **knowing and understanding that information can be represented in a number of different forms, including graphics, sounds and texts;**
- **being able to describe the processes of investigation, which can involve exploring and discovering phenomena and events, proposing explanations, initiating investigations, predicting outcomes, testing, modifying and applying understanding.**

We should also expect that in science children will be moving towards being able to:

- **present confidently oral reports about topics they have investigated;**
- **take part in classroom debates about scientific issues;**
- **participate actively in classroom discussion about science topics and investigations;**
- **interpret a variety of forms of information;**
- **predict outcomes, and generate hypotheses and explanations related to scientific phenomena;**
- **suggest cause-and-effect relationships in explaining a set of observations;**
- **formulate an explanation for a set of observations;**
- **organise complex information, ideas and arguments, using a variety of media;**
- **select, summarise and organise ideas and information from a variety of sources;**
- **use complex drawings, tables and graphs to organise and retrieve information;**
- **appreciate the need for careful assessment of science reports in the media.**

Generally, children will need explicit teaching if they are to understand the literacy demands of science.

Supporting children as learners

Children become literate as they use language to interact with peers, teachers and the wider school community in many contexts. Therefore, they should have many opportunities to interact with others, to express feelings and opinions and to listen and respond to the views of others. They should have experiences with a wide range of texts. In all subjects, children develop understandings and learn new concepts and skills through the use of language. As they explore their environment, investigate problems and participate in co-operative learning activities, they use language to clarify their thinking, to share and test ideas, to communicate with others and to reflect on their own learning and respond to what they hear and see.

Learning experiences should be designed to involve children in speaking and listening, reading and writing a variety of texts which relate closely to real-world purposes. As an example, consider the group task: *Use cardboard to build a bridge which will bear a two kilogram weight.* In this activity children have to collaborate in planning and carrying out tasks, gathering background information (perhaps on materials, shapes and bridge design), design and construct one or more models, design and evaluate experimental tests on these models and present written and oral reports. Through these activities children will be engaged in describing, instructing, explaining and arguing, using oral and written text forms.

Children should have opportunities to become confident in speaking and writing in a variety of contexts. They should be encouraged to experiment with and explore ways of expressing ideas and communicating meaning as they develop their skills in writing for various purposes and audiences. They should be helped to develop as independent learners as they use language to make their meanings clear to themselves and others. In order to understand how language works, children should talk frequently about the written and spoken texts with which they are working. They should have many opportunities to read, write, talk and listen and to focus on the grammatical features that successful texts employ (e.g. recognising that verbs begin sentences in effective instructions). In this way children will develop a 'shared language' for describing the way language works to achieve particular purposes in science. Learning experiences should provide models of successful texts and opportunities for children to create their own texts with support as they move towards independence. There should be frequent opportunities for children to participate with their teachers and other learners in the joint construction of texts, before they are encouraged to create texts alone.

For children to be successful in science, opportunities need to be provided to understand and use a variety of text forms. Thus, after practical work in science children should be asked to write simple instructions, reports, recounts and explanations as well as other more complex forms of experimental records. These complex forms could include entries in a personal learning journal or a more traditional experimental report. The learning activities in science should be designed around real texts. Authentic texts, both spoken and written, form a context for teaching about science, about how language works and provide a framework for learning science knowledge. These texts will be in forms such as science textbooks, reference books, videos/DVDs, popular science magazines, some internet sites, selected newspaper articles, zoo and museum guides.

Approaches to teaching

Your teaching of the literacy of science should involve the following sequence.

1. *Determining prior knowledge,* where you use a variety of ways to find out what prior knowledge and understanding of language and science children bring to a new topic area. In the process of doing this you also help activate the prior knowledge the children have, which will help them use this knowledge to make sense of new ideas.

2. *Interacting with texts,* where you help the children locate, read and make sense of texts relevant to the topic they are studying.

3. *Modelling,* where you work together with the children on texts which demonstrate the text type on which you are focusing. You can deconstruct texts, giving children the chance to discuss them and pointing out such things as the relationship between author and reader, the channel of communication (usually speaking or writing), and the language features and the structure of the text. During this phase, children will begin to build up a language for analysing and discussing texts which they can apply to other texts of the same type.

4. *Collaborative and scaffolded construction of texts.* Children can now begin to construct their own texts because they have gained understanding of the text from the previous phase. They will need to carry out research to build further knowledge. You can then guide and assist with the construction of the text, working with the whole class, with small groups or with individuals. Some children will benefit from further scaffolded support using such devices as planning and writing frames to guide their speaking and writing.

5. *Independent construction of texts.* You can now allow children to develop their own texts. They will need to carry out research for the new writing. Encourage them to discuss their drafts with other children and with you before revising and editing in preparation for publication.

Applying the teaching sequence

The application of the various phases of the teaching sequence just briefly described will be illustrated by a classroom example. The activities described relate to a project on water and the activities were used with a mixed class of Years 5 and 6 children.

Determining prior knowledge

The first step was to establish some of what the children already knew about water. To do this, their teacher asked them to work in pairs to complete a structured concept map about water. The blank concept map she used is shown in Figure 6.1 and the concept map produced by one pair is shown in Figure 6.2.

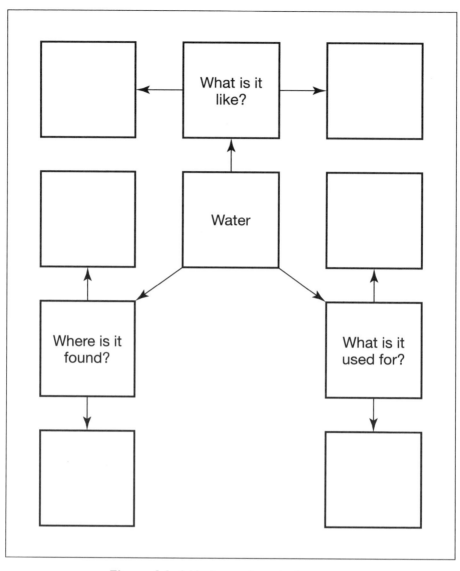

Figure 6.1 *A blank concept map about water*

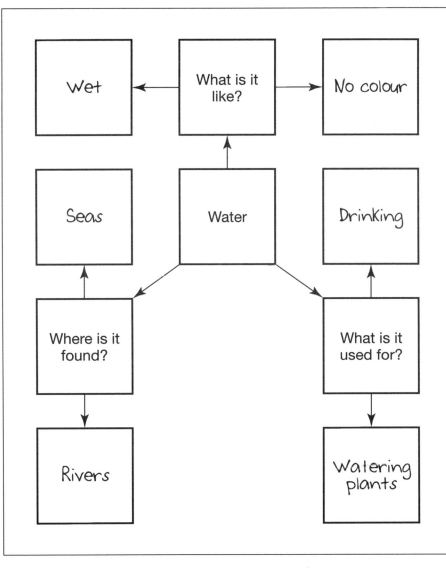

Figure 6.2 *A completed concept map about water*

Interacting with texts

The next step was to work with the children on a text that would give them further information about this topic. One suitable text is given in Figure 6.3.

Water around us

Water <u>is</u> a naturally occurring substance. It <u>has</u> special properties which <u>make</u> it very important to life.

Water is colourless, odourless and tasteless in its pure form. Most water on Earth is in the liquid state, but it also may occur as a solid called *ice* and as a gas called *water vapour*.

Water occurs in many places on Earth. The total amount of water on Earth is about 1.5 million million million litres. About 97 per cent of this is found in the oceans as salt water. Another 2 per cent occurs in frozen form, mostly in glaciers and in the polar ice caps. The remaining 1 per cent is underground, in lakes and rivers, and in the atmosphere.

Water is very important to people and has many uses. It makes up about 65 per cent of the human body. Water is used up in our bodies, so we need to drink at least 2 litres of water each day. In the home, water is used for cooking, cleaning and washing. It is drunk also by animals and used to grow plants in home gardens and on farms. In industry it is used for such purposes as cooling machines, transporting goods and making electricity.

Figure 6.3 *Water around us*

The teacher asked the children to work in pairs to suggest answers to the questions listed in Figure 6.4.

---

1. Why did someone write this text?
2. Who do you think wrote the text and who did they write it for?
3. The first paragraph is a general statement that introduces what the text will be about. Label it as *Classification*. The next three paragraphs describe different aspects of water. Match each of the following labels to the other paragraphs and write them next to the right paragraph:

   Description – uses   *Description – appearance*   *Description – occurrence*
4. The verbs in paragraph 1 have been underlined. Underline the verbs in the other paragraphs. What tense are they?
5. A paragraph often begins with a sentence which previews the rest of the information written in that paragraph. Underline the sentence in each paragraph which previews the rest of that paragraph.

Figure 6.4 *Questions about text structure and features*

Notice how these questions focus the children's attention on the structure of the text they are reading and on the important language features of that kind of text. In the terms used to describe text types in Chapter 2, this is a report text.

Modelling

The teacher then went on to help the children make sense of the text they were studying. This was done through a shared reading activity using the text featured in Figure 6.3. This text is shown again in Figure 6.5, where the left-hand column shows the text that was presented to the children on an overhead projector transparency, and read aloud with them (with teacher and children sharing the reading). In the right-hand column you can see part of the commentary the teacher made about this text as she read it with the class.

Water is a naturally occurring substance. It has special properties which make it very important to life.	*This is the introduction paragraph. It tells me what the text will be about and gives me some clues about what it will say.*	1
	I wonder what it means by 'naturally occurring'? I know that if something occurs, it happens, so may it means that water happens naturally. That would mean that nobody actually deliberately makes it.	2
Water is colourless, odourless and tasteless in its pure form. Most water on Earth is in the liquid state, but it also may occur as a solid called *ice* and as a gas called *water vapour*.	*So water has no colour, no odour (which I think means smell) and no taste. That's funny because the water you get in bottles from the supermarket definitely tastes different to the water from the tap. So how can it say that it has no taste? It does say 'in its pure form' so maybe the water in bottles or from the tap is not actually pure. I remember being told that they do put chemicals into tap water, to kill the germs, so maybe it isn't pure.*	3
Water occurs in many places on Earth. The total amount of water on Earth is about 1.5 million million million litres. About 97 per cent of this is found in the oceans as salt water. Another 2 per cent occurs in frozen form, mostly in glaciers and in the polar ice caps. The remaining 1 per cent is underground, in lakes and rivers, and in the atmosphere.	*I know that there is water in seas and rivers. I wonder what other places it is found in? So, in oceans, yes: frozen in glaciers and ice, and underground as well. I didn't think of those last two places. But most of it is in the oceans, isn't it?*	4
Water is very important to people and has many uses. It makes up about 65 per cent of the human body. Water is used up in our bodies, so we need to drink at least 2 litres of water each day. In the home, water is used for cooking, cleaning and washing. It is drunk also by animals and used to grow plants in home gardens and on farms. In industry it is used for such purposes as cooling machines, transporting goods and making electricity.		

Figure 6.5 *Part of a shared read of a text about water*

Notice how, in her commentary, the teacher thinks aloud to the children, giving them access to her thought processes as she reads the text. She demonstrates for them how she:

- **figures out the structure of the text she is reading and what the significance of that structure is;**
- **works out a possible meaning for a term she initially does not know;**
- **creates meaning from the text by the clever combining of her existing background knowledge and new information given by the text;**
- **asks herself questions about the text which then guides the way she reads it.**

These are all important strategies for understanding what you read and the teacher will almost certainly have introduced these to her children as part of shared reading in her literacy teaching. Here she reinforces these strategies and demonstrates their use in a different curriculum context.

Collaborative and scaffolded construction of texts

The teacher then moved on to help the children write their own examples of report texts using the information they had learned about water, and the understandings they had gained about the structure of this kind of text.

She firstly did a shared writing activity with them using the outline framework shown in Figure 6.6. During this activity, the teacher asked for suggestions from the class and then wrote into the framework herself again, using an overhead transparency version (using an interactive whiteboard for this would have been even more effective).

Title: **Water in our world**
Classification: **What is water?**
Description: **What do we know about the appearance of water?**
Description: **Where do we find water?**
Description: **What are the uses of water?**

Figure 6.6 *An outline framework for writing about water*

Then, to help the children put these ideas into a connected and well structured report, the teacher gave each pair of children a copy of the blank writing frame shown in Figure 6.7.

Water in our world
Water is
It is also
Here are some important facts about the appearance of water.
Firstly
Secondly
Water is found in a number of places.
Most of the water in our world is found in
Water is also found in
and in
We use water in a number of ways.
We
We also
The most interesting thing about water is

Figure 6.7 *A writing frame for writing about water*

Independent construction of texts

Children will need to be taken through the teaching sequence above several times so that they become thoroughly familiar with the structure of a report text. As they work, it is helpful to gradually remove some of the support you have offered them. One time, for example, you might ask them to write reports using an outline framework like that in Figure 6.6, and deliberately not offer them a full writing frame. At a later stage they might not even need the outline framework, or might simply need to be reminded of it.

What you are doing here is gradually weaning them off the support systems that you offer so that they can write more and more independently.

Summary

In this chapter we have considered the crucial role of literacy in the learning of science and showed how you might develop teaching approaches to furthering children's expertise in using literacy in this subject area. You should have noticed that, even though we have focused here on literacy skills, all the time there is still a heavy emphasis on the content that is being learnt – that is, the science. To repeat what I have claimed earlier, integrating literacy teaching into subject teaching produces a win–win situation. Children develop their literacy but they also develop their knowledge and understanding in the subject.

References and further reading

Wellington, J and Osborne, J (2001) *Language and literacy in science education.* Buckingham: Open University Press. This very accessible book explores the main difficulties in the language of science and examines practical ways to aid children in retaining, understanding, reading, speaking and writing scientific language. The authors draw together and synthesise current good practice, thinking and research in this field. They use many practical examples and illustrations to exemplify principles and to provide guidelines in developing language and literacy in the learning of science. They also consider the impact that the growing use of information and communications technology has had, and will have, on writing, reading and information handling in science lessons.

7 LITERACY ACROSS THE PRIMARY CURRICULUM: LOOKING AT MATHEMATICS

Chapter objectives:

The aim of this chapter is to introduce you to:
- *the place of literacy within mathematics and the text types which are characteristic of this curriculum subject;*
- *an approach to developing literacy, and particularly writing, within mathematics.*

Introduction

I made the point in the previous chapter that children use literacy all the time in science lessons. Mathematics lessons are no different, although there are clearly differences in the kinds of texts children will encounter and the kinds of skills they will be expected to use. Of course, the principal purpose of text in mathematics will usually be to record the working out of mathematical problems and will probably feature the writing of numbers rather than letters. There are other purposes, however, and there needs to be an enhanced role for literacy within the teaching and learning of mathematics. Some of these purposes might be:

- **to plan and record mathematical investigations;**
- **to predict mathematical outcomes;**
- **to recount mathematical work of various kinds, including calculations;**
- **to give instructions for carrying out mathematical procedures;**
- **to offer a detailed proof of a mathematical phenomenon.**

As in the previous chapter, I will examine the four language modes of talking, listening, reading and writing to uncover some of the ways these are important in the learning of mathematics. Before I do that, it would be useful for you to undertake the following task.

Practical task

Language in mathematics

Observe a mathematics lesson taught by another teacher in your school setting. Using the following grid format, make some brief notes to record any instances you see of children using talking, listening, reading or writing to engage with the mathematics content of the lesson. As an example, I have completed the first observation, which relates to a ficticious but realistic mathematics lesson.

Language mode used (talking, listening, reading or writing)	Context of use (whole-class work, group work, individual work, using book exercises, using concrete materials, etc.)	Mathematical content
Reading, listening, talking	*Whole-class session. Teacher presented several written problems on the whiteboard. Children read each one, talked in pairs about what mathematical calculation would be involved in solving this problem. Teacher discussed each one with them and wrote on the whiteboard the problem in mathematical form. They then worked through the 'sum' in class discussion.*	*Four rules of number. Identifying maths problems within connected text.*

Write down any observations you have as a result of this activity about the role of language in mathematics teaching.

Language in mathematics

Talking

In studying mathematics children are expected to:

- discuss;
- explain;
- describe;
- argue a particular point of view (for example, justify a strategy for solving a problem).

The learning of mathematics relies heavily on oral and written explanations. Working in small, collaborative groups, children can be given the opportunity to communicate orally, join in discussions constructively, and express ideas and opinions without dominating. This may help them to make the link between language and meaning.

By encouraging children to talk, you can assess the link between the children's previous understanding of mathematics and the new concepts being introduced. Discussions between the teacher and children can also be beneficial as a preparation for reading or writing activities, since they can help activate children's understanding before they undertake the task.

Asking children to present a verbal report to the class also provides an opportunity for children to choose an appropriate language form for the audience.

Listening

When studying mathematics, children are expected to listen in order to gain information and follow instructions. This means that they will have opportunities to ask questions (of the teacher and their peers) to clarify meanings, to respond to alternative viewpoints, and to make brief notes based on a spoken explanation. While children are listening, the teacher could write on the board words that may cause difficulties. Words that may be misinterpreted because of the similarity of their sounds include *ankle* for *angle*, and *size* for *sides*.

Reading

In studying mathematics, children are expected to read to locate specific information, and understand concepts and procedures, as well as to interpret problems.

When we read familiar texts we often skip over some words, change their order or even substitute other words. Language is normally full of redundant information. This allows us to understand by skimming rather than intensive reading or to gain meaning from the use of key words and contextual clues. Mathematics texts, however, are often much denser than texts in other subjects. This means that few words are used, all essential to the meaning. Consequently, as part of the literacy demands of mathematics, word order is very important.

Consider the following two questions which contain exactly the same words.

- *Sixty is half of what number?*
- *Half of sixty is what number?*

Apparently otherwise insignificant small words such as *to*, *of* or *by* become vitally important for making sense in mathematics. Compare 'increase by one-third' to 'increase to one-third'.

Similarly, the description of change is often dependent on the use of prepositions.

- *The temperature increased to 5 degrees.*
- *The temperature increased by 5 degrees.*
- *The temperature increased from 5 degrees.*

The demands in processing such language are often far more complex than the underlying number facts suggest. The following question demonstrates this difficulty.

> *Mary is 35 years younger than Tom. Fred is half the age of Mary. Judy is 17 years older than Fred. If Judy is 35, how old is Tom?*

Each sentence is short and compares the ages of two people. The comparisons are *younger than, half the age of* and *older than*. Beyond the use of three different comparisons, the order of reference of the people presented in pairs is intentionally designed to increase the difficulty of the question.

Children can use several strategies when reading difficult texts. These include talking to others about information in the text, re-reading parts of the question, making notes about key features, using diagrams which accompany the text or using diagrams to make sense of the text.

The order in which information is presented in language is often at odds with the order in which it is processed in mathematics. This mismatch occurs even with very simple instructions such as 'Take 6 from 12'. Weaker readers will often process information in the order in which it is encountered. Even children fluent in everyday spoken English may still have problems with 'The number 5 is 2 less than what number?'. The *5, 2* and *less* in that order suggest the answer is *3*. The way the words are put together (the syntax) produces a different result. The mental restructuring that is necessary to get this meaning may overload a child's processing and memory capabilities. Children often give up and simply guess what to do with the numbers.

Confusion over the order for processing information in text may lead to inappropriate simplifying strategies. This is common with children attempting division questions. There is no consistent left-to-right processing of meaning in English.

- *What is 3 divided by 6?*
- *Divide 3 into 6.*
- *Divide 3 into 6 equal parts.*

Furthermore, this lack of 'order' is perpetuated by two different symbolic orders.

- **3 ÷ 6.**
- **6/3.**

Little wonder children create for themselves a rule of 'always divide the small number into the big number'.

'More' or 'less'

Look at the following three questions, each of which involves the numbers 3 and 5, and uses the relation 'more than'.

- *Which number is three more than five?*
- *Five is how many more than three?*
- *Five is three more than which number?*

In the first question the *three* and *five* are separated by *more than* and the answer is the sum of 3 and 5. This agrees with a 'key mathematical vocabulary' approach common in teaching that links the phrase *more than* to addition. A child applying this approach to the second and third questions would be surprised to find that the answers have changed.

A 'key mathematical vocabulary' approach to address the literacy demands of mathematics may be counterproductive. Yet this approach is commonly used to attempt to overcome literacy problems. After all, *more than* sometimes does mean addition. But it does not always, and knowing when to apply which meaning of the term is a fairly sophisticated literacy skill, which needs teaching. Contrary to the belief that mathematics makes less use of language than other subjects, you can see that mathematics has its own subject-specific language structures.

Writing

In mathematics, children are expected to write when they answer questions and present proofs, and to consolidate understanding. Many forms of writing can be undertaken in mathematics, such as writing proofs and solving algebraic problems. As children write, they will decide when help is needed. They may then approach a friend for an idea, or a dictionary for the best word or spelling. They also re-read their work during writing to maintain meaning, change words and phrases, or check for errors. It is useful for children to learn to emphasise those parts of the text or question that are causing them difficulties. This could include underlining, circling or highlighting words, and understanding why some words are written in bold, or in a different typeface. Encourage children to ask questions, so they can clarify and consolidate what they are learning. You should also encourage activities which require discussion with others and which include making notes, lists or drawing diagrams. This allows children to apply the concepts they have learned and to reflect on their work.

In the rest of this chapter I want to explore in rather more detail the characteristics of written mathematical texts and what might be expected of learners in the subject. I will go on to suggest approaches to teaching writing within mathematics.

Research insight

Writing in mathematics

Candia Morgan has produced an extremely thorough review of the research literature on the relationship between learning mathematics and writing (Morgan, 1998), upon which several of the ideas in this section of this chapter are based. Morgan's work focuses largely on secondary school mathematics and she herself admits that there is little actual research into the writing that primary children produce in mathematics. Nevertheless, her analysis has many strong implications for primary school mathematics, and I will explore some of these in what follows.

The mathematics register

Very mention of the term 'the language of mathematics' suggests that there is a single set of characteristics which can be listed and applied. This is rather simplistic. Just as there are a number of activities that can be labelled as mathematics (including academic mathematics, school mathematics, recreational mathematics, etc.), there is a variety of genres of text that may be called mathematical (e.g. a research paper, a textbook, an examination question and answer, a puzzle, etc.). Each of these activities and genres will have some distinctive characteristics of its own and there are, for example, some features of the genre of academic mathematics research papers that we would be surprised to see appear in a primary child's report of some investigative work. It seems likely, however, that any text that is identifiable as mathematical will share at least some linguistic characteristics with other texts that are also considered to be mathematical.

The linguistic features that contribute to identifying a text as mathematical include its vocabulary, its grammatical structure and the forms of argument it uses. A number of authors have given descriptions of the general features of mathematical texts. Halliday (1974) introduced the use of the concept of a mathematical 'register' to discussions about language in mathematics education contexts and provided an overview of some of the grammatical characteristics of such a register.

The most obvious characteristic is the use of a symbolic system completely different from that found in everyday written English. Many mathematical texts are full of 'sentences' like:

$$(a^2 + b^2)/3c = \sqrt{(x - y)} + z^2$$

This feature has led to the language of mathematics being described as 'a foreign language' (Ervinck, 1992) and, when it is combined with the use of specialist vocabulary to name specifically mathematical objects and concepts (*radius, sum, integer, tangent, hypotenuse*), it is not surprising that learners find the reading and writing of mathematical text difficult. While symbols and specialist vocabulary are perhaps the most visible aspects of many mathematical texts, they do not provide a full description of the nature of these texts. It is also necessary to look beyond the level of vocabulary to the syntax of the text and to the structures which serve to construct mathematical arguments.

Other features that have been identified as characteristic of much mathematical language include its 'density and conciseness ... which tend to concentrate the reader's attention on the correctness of what was written rather than on its richness of meaning' (Austin and Howson, 1979, p. 174). Like the scientific texts discussed in the previous chapter, mathematics texts in general have a high 'lexical density', that is, a high ratio of 'content' words to 'grammatical' words.

Mathematics language also uses distinctive grammatical structures such as conditional phrases ('if ... then ...'), and hypothetical imperatives ('Let $a = 3$ ...'), one of the problems with which is the difference in usage and meaning of these structures from that found in everyday language. Readers and writers of mathematical text need firstly to 'tune in' to the genre, that is, recognise it as different from their normal language.

Mathematics texts

There are, of course, many differences between the forms of language used in different mathematical contexts, and it is not clear that the idea of a single mathematical register can cover the variation of functions and meanings to be found, for example, in a primary school textbook and in an academic research paper. Not only does the subject matter vary but the modes of argument used in these different areas of mathematical activity are likely to differ substantially. Yet one of the aims of school mathematics teaching is to produce learners who, eventually, can understand and produce the mathematics writing that mathematicians deal with. So, what does this writing look like?

Academic mathematics texts

The academic mathematics research report may be seen as the 'adult' equivalent of the investigation report. Even though mathematics writing is closely identified with a distinct symbol system, most guidelines and advice for writers of mathematics suggest that some 'natural language' is required to supplement the symbols (e.g. Gillman, 1987; Knuth et al., 1989). The reasons given by these authors for including non-symbolic elements in mathematical texts, however, suggest that they are chiefly to make the text easier to read, particularly to an audience beyond the very small group of colleagues working in the same field, rather than to contribute to its meaning.

It is generally accepted that both scientific and mathematical texts are impersonal and formal. Clearly, the symbolic content discussed above contributes to this, but there are also a number of contributory characteristics of the 'natural' language, such as high modality (i.e. a high degree of certainty and an absence of such human characteristics as doubt or expressions of attitude). It would be unusual, for example, in a mathematics text to read the statement, *I think the answer to the question 23 $\times$ 4 is 92. This may be because four 20s might make 80, and you perhaps have to add four 3s, which could be 12. So 80 added to 12 is likely to be 92.* The use of language like this in, say, a personal response to a poem in English would not be remarkable at all.

Another source of this formality, as with science texts, is the use of nominal rather than verbal expressions. Look at the following statement, which is written in formal mathematical language:

The demand that one angle of the isosceles triangle be equal to 90° means that ...

Compare it with the following, which is in more everyday language:

I want to make one angle of the isosceles triangle equal to 90°, and this means that ...

The use of nominalisation in the first sentence means that the reader is separated from the source of the 'demand'. This is represented as an abstract entity whose independent existence has important consequences. The ability to represent processes as objects and hence to operate on the processes/objects themselves is part of the power of mathematics but, at the same time, it increases the impersonal effect, strengthening the impression that it is these processes/objects that are the active participants in mathematics rather than human mathematicians.

Looking beyond the level of individual symbols, words or even more complex phrases or statements, it is also the case that the structures of texts, in particular the ways in which arguments are constructed, are distinctive in mathematics. In academic mathematics a very high value is placed on deductive reasoning as a means of both 'discovering' knowledge and providing evidence for it. The linguistic structure of mathematical texts reflects this, especially in texts such as formal mathematical proofs. This text type is a standard component of most formal mathematical texts above school level (and in some school texts as well) but does cause even advanced learners considerable difficulty. In analysing the structure of proofs, writers (e.g. Konior, 1993) have pointed out the importance of linguistic signals which mark the beginning (*It remains to show that ...*) and end (*Whence formula (24) follows ...*) of phases in the argument. Konior suggests that expert readers make use of these signals to structure their reading of the whole text, but that non-experts may not appreciate the function of such phrases. Equally it is likely that non-expert mathematical writers may not know how to make use of them effectively to create such texts.

The characteristics of academic mathematical texts briefly outlined above form part of the background to the consideration of mathematical writing in school. While schoolchildren themselves are unlikely to come across such texts, they do form part of the experience of mathematics teachers and textbook writers and, as such, influence the texts encountered by children in school and the values placed by teachers on various forms of writing.

School mathematics texts

School mathematics texts have been thoroughly examined in terms of the difficulties they create for children in understanding their meanings.

Although it is possible to criticise the conciseness and formality of mathematics textbooks because of the difficulties that they may cause learners, it is also the case that such books form a very large part of most children's (and their teachers') experience of mathematical text. Characteristics of their language are likely, therefore, to influence children's writing in mathematics.

Like academic mathematical texts, school texts have a heavy symbolic content, although the range of symbols they contain is likely to be more limited. In addition, most school mathematics texts are heavily graphical and include tables, graphs, diagrams, plans, maps and pictures. It is probably the case, however, that these graphical elements are mostly 'decorative' (Shuard and Rothery, 1984, p. 47) rather than 'mathematical'.

Research insight

Reading in mathematics

Hilary Shuard and Andrew Rothery's (1984) classic study identified difficulties associated with the use in mathematical textbooks of graphical elements, with the layout of their pages, as well as with their vocabulary and symbolism, any of which might contribute to a child's inability to make sense of the mathematics within them. Shuard and Rothery also looked closely at the differences between everyday and mathematical English. They categorised the words used in mathematics into three distinctive groups. The first group contained words exclusive to the subject of mathematics, e.g. square root. The second group contained words found in everyday English and in mathematics but in each case their meanings are different, e.g. difference, prime and similar. The third group contained words used in both contexts with more or less the same meanings. Their conclusion was that reading in mathematics was not at all a simple matter.

Such decorative features are also characteristic of the text in school mathematics books, as well as the graphics. As Kane (1968) points out, school texts tend to use a conventional and repetitive structure, in particular those sections containing examples and exercises. One of the effects of this, which may well be deliberate on the part of textbook producers, is to make the mathematics in the books easily accessible to children, without them being distracted by having to decipher unfamiliar text structures before getting to the mathematics. While this undoubtedly eases teachers' lives (children who grasp quickly what they have to do are less likely to ask irritating questions), it does little to induct children into the typical characteristics of mathematics writing.

As we saw with science in the previous chapter, there are some distinctive characteristics of mathematics writing with which we would hope that our children, eventually, become familiar. Again, as with science, writing in mathematics is closely bound up with learning mathematics and the development of mathematical literacy. Developing children's ability requires explicit teaching of the conventional structures of mathematical writing and a range of exemplars of good practice. Given the remarks above about school mathematics texts, it is unlikely that experience of these alone will be sufficient to produce children who can move towards writing mathematics like mathematicians. For this, they need more targeted teaching.

Before exploring strategies for accomplishing this, we need to spend a little time looking at another important line of development in thinking about the role of writing in mathematics. It has been suggested that, in mathematics as in other subjects, writing in a subject is an important means of learning in that subject.

Practical task

Looking at mathematics textbooks

Choose a mathematics textbook which is currently used in the school in which you are based. Have a careful look at the nature of the text contained in this book, using the following questions to guide you.

1. *Can you find any use of graphical elements in the book which you think might be confusing to your children? (Think about icons. Some texts, for example, have icons such as ☜ which might mean 'look carefully at this', or ✐ which might mean 'you need to write something down here'. Are these meanings obvious?)*

2. *Can you find any examples of vocabulary whose meaning might be ambiguous? (Think about terms such as share, difference, round, which might mean something different in everyday English to their intended meaning in the mathematics book.)*

3. *Can you find any examples of 'decorative' features? (Think about pictures, etc., which seem to be there simply to break up the page or make it look jolly. Think also about decorative language – that is, language which, if you removed it entirely, would not make too much difference to the meaning of what is written.)*

In the light of what you have found, how far would you consider this text 'readable' for the children you teach? What might get in the way of this readability? What might enhance it?

Writing to learn in the mathematics classroom

Recent years have seen an increasing interest in communication in the mathematics classroom. In tandem with the move towards constructivist views of learning, children have begun to be given a role as producers of mathematical language rather than just as consumers. Attention has moved towards consideration of the roles that talking and writing may play in children's learning of mathematics.

The role of talking in learning mathematics has received a good deal of attention, with many suggestions for ways that teachers might encourage talk in their classrooms (e.g. Brissenden, 1988; Mathematical Association, 1987). The place of writing, however, is rather less well established. Supporters of 'writing-to-learn' in mathematics have suggested that writing should be part of investigations, claiming that writing can help children in their learning of mathematics, in particular in developing reflection and problem-solving processes.

Traditionally, very little writing, other than symbolic notation, has taken place in mathematics classrooms. The classic studies of writing in secondary classrooms in England and Wales (Britton et al., 1975; Martin et al., 1976) and in Scotland (Rogers and MacDonald, 1985) found that there was so little writing taking place in mathematics lessons that it was hardly worth analysing. These studies are dated but they do indicate the lack of independent mathematical writing in secondary classrooms.

Evidence from primary schools is even harder to come by and the only readily available evidence about the nature of writing in primary school mathematics lessons comes from an Australian study (Marks and Mousley, 1990). This found a very limited range of writing being used and, even where teachers claimed to be committed to the idea of increasing opportunities for their children to use language in the classroom to develop and communicate their mathematical understanding, children generally only wrote recounts (see Chapter 2 for a full description of this text type) rather than specifically mathematical styles. That is, they wrote saying what they had done in their mathematics investigations, rather than trying to analyse or explain what they found.

More recently there has been a development from the idea of 'writing across the curriculum', which focused on the development of writing through its use in various curriculum areas, towards the idea that writing is a useful tool for helping learning in all areas of the curriculum. Writing is seen to share a number of the characteristics of successful learning: that is, it integrates hand, eye and brain in the quest to represent reality; it compels the reformulation of ideas ('thinking at the point of utterance' in James Britton's words); and it is audience focused. As the writer struggles to represent ideas in a manner which an outside reader can understand, he/she is forced to clarify these ideas for him/herself. Writing is thus 'epistemic': it creates knowledge in the writer.

Some researchers have seen a special relationship between writing and mathematics. Emig (1983) defines 'clear writing' as:

> that which signals without ambiguity the nature of conceptual relationships, whether they be coordinate, subordinate, superordinate, causal, or something other. (p. 127)

Such a concern with precision and with relationships seems to fit naturally within mathematics.

Research insight

Writing and learning in mathematics

There is some evidence to support the relationship between writing and learning in mathematics. In one study (Williams, 2003), for example, secondary children were placed in control and experimental groups for the purpose of researching writing and problem-solving. Each group was taught a number of mathematical strategies and processes, and they were then each given problems to complete. The experimental group was asked in addition to write a few sentences about how they solved their problems; the control group was not required to write about their processes at all. The results showed that the children in both groups made progress in mathematical problem-solving, but that the children in the experimental group had learnt to solve the problems using more appropriate strategies at a faster rate than children in the control group. Being forced to express their thinking in writing seemed to have helped the children in the experimental group to understand the mathematics they were engaged with.

In addition to claims that writing can enhance learning in a subject like mathematics, another potentially important reason for enhancing the role of writing is that it might improve children's attitudes towards mathematics and perhaps lessen one of the major obstacles to their learning. Some writers (e.g. Borasi and Rose, 1989) have suggested that writing texts such as journals can help change children's perceptions of mathematics away from a simple 'search for the right answer' towards a more satisfying problem-solving attitude.

What might children write in mathematics?

Several teachers and researchers have suggested that writing should play a greater role in classroom mathematics work. There is little agreement, however, about what exactly children should write and there has, in fact, been little research analysing the kinds of texts which do get written in mathematics lessons, particularly in primary schools. I earlier suggested that children might be expected to use written language:

- **to plan and record mathematical investigations;**
- **to predict mathematical outcomes;**
- **to recount mathematical work of various kinds, including calculations;**
- **to give instructions for carrying out mathematical procedures;**
- **to offer a detailed proof of a mathematical phenomenon.**

All of these text types have distinctive structures and language features, and it would be unreasonable to expect children simply to pick these up. The need for teaching is clear.

Teaching writing in mathematics

Your teaching of the literacy of mathematics should involve the same sequence of activities that we explored in the previous chapter in relation to the teaching of literacy in science.

1. *Determining prior knowledge*, where you use a variety of ways to find out what prior knowledge and understanding of language and mathematics children bring to a new topic area.

2. *Interacting with texts*, where you help your children locate, read and make sense of texts relevant to the topic they are studying.

3. *Modelling*, where you work together with your children on texts which demonstrate the text type on which you are focusing.

4. *Collaborative and scaffolded construction of texts*. Children can now begin to construct their own texts because they have gained understanding of the text from the previous phase.

5. *Independent construction of texts*. You can now allow children to develop their own texts.

Applying the teaching sequence

Determining prior knowledge

One useful strategy for gaining an insight into the previous knowledge of a group of children is to work with them on a disrupted text. The example given in Figure 7.1 uses what is usually known as a cloze text for this purpose.

Ordering numbers

Numbers can be written in ascending or _____ order.

    If numbers are written in ascending _____ that means that the smallest number is _____. The rest of the numbers get _____ and _____. The largest number is always _____. The numbers 35, 53 and 103 are written in _____ order. If the numbers 820, 280, 802 and 208 are written in ascending order then this is the order in which they would be: _____, 280, _____, and _____.

    When numbers are written in descending order then the largest _____ is always first. The rest of the numbers get _____ and _____. These numbers are in _____ order: 153, 150, 103, 53. If I write the numbers 418, 483, 438 and 348 in descending order, this would be the order in which they would be: _____, 438, _____, _____.

Figure 7.1 *Ordering numbers*

This text can be used in a shared reading activity with a class or group, or as a guided reading activity with children working in pairs or threes.

Interacting with texts

One way of getting children to search for information relevant to a particular topic is to provide them with a grid to guide their reading. One teacher used the grid in Figure 7.2 with her Year 4 class to focus their search for information about regular two-dimensional shapes.

	How many sides does this shape have?	How many corners are there inside the shape (angles)	Does this shape tessellate?
Triangle			
Rectangle			
Pentagon			
Hexagon			
Octagon			

Figure 7.2 *A search grid for 2-D shapes*

Modelling

Figure 7.3 shows a text which you might find useful for shared reading with Years 4–6 children.

History of number

The history of number begins with early humans, who did not have a complex number system. Complex number systems developed as the need for large numbers grew.

One early system was the Roman number system. This is still used today on some watches and clocks.

In the Roman system, if a smaller unit appears before a larger one, it is subtracted from the larger one, for example V = 5, I = 1 so IV = 4.

Here are some of the symbols the Romans used.

1	I	one finger
5	V	one hand
10	X	two Vs
50	L	half a C
100	C	centum = hundred

A third system is the Hindu-Arabic system. This was invented by the Hindus around 300BC. In this number system the position of a symbol (number) is very important and a zero is used instead of using an empty space. Hindu-Arabic symbols are what we use today.

Figure 7.3 *A shared reading text about the history of numbers*

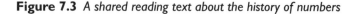

Practical task

Shared reading with a mathematics text

Use the text given in Figure 7.3 as a shared reading text in a mathematics lesson.

Before you use the text, go through it and mark points at which you might want to 'think aloud' your reading processes. Here are some ideas to get you started.

Paragraph 1: How might you work out what the word 'complex' means? It is clearly something to do with larger numbers. What kind of number system might do for small numbers? Probably quite a simple one, so perhaps 'complex' means the opposite of simple?

Paragraph 3: So IV means 4 because it is 5 (V) – 1 (I). So IX must be 10 (X) – 1 (I), that's 9. I wonder if IC is 100 (C) – 1 (I), or 99?

Collaborative and scaffolded construction of texts

It will also be useful for you to exemplify mathematical writing by composing examples in shared writing sessions. A useful time to demonstrate investigative report writing, for example, would be after a group have completed an investigation in mathematics and are going on to write their own reports about this. You can, with help from the children, compose an example report on an overhead projector or interactive whiteboard. In the course of this you can discuss several important points.

- **How should the report begin?**
- **What tense should it use?**
- **Should it mention the people who carried out the investigation by name, or should it talk about 'we'? Are there other ways of recounting what happened? What about using the passive?**
- **How should the report be structured? Should it use numbered sections, bullet points, or simple paragraphs?**
- **At which point should the report say what the investigation found?**

Children will also benefit from some scaffolding support for their mathematics writing. Figure 7.4 shows a writing frame which some children might find useful for structuring their writing in advance of carrying out an investigation.

Mathematics: Planning and prediction

I have been asked to investigate

I already know that

So I will investigate by

I think I will find that

Figure 7.4 *A mathematics writing frame*

Independent construction of texts

Obviously children will vary in how long it takes them to move to independent construction of texts in mathematics. Some will need to reply on scaffolds and frames for much longer than others. Do try to make sure, however, that you constantly look for opportunities to move all your children on in their capabilities. Many will produce excellent writing using frames, for example, but they do need, probably sooner rather than later, to be weaned off these supports to become independent writers, and this requires some deliberateness in approach.

Summary

In this chapter I have explored the nature of writing in a number of mathematical contexts. While many mathematics teachers are suspicious about focusing upon children's writing in their subject, there is sufficient evidence available to suggest that this could be a beneficial move, not least in the support which writing in a subject gives to learning in that subject.

Mathematics writing is not natural: it needs teaching if children eventually are to be able to write in a manner approximating that of mathematicians. I have argued in this chapter that teaching writing in mathematics is no different from teaching writing in any subject, and aspects of the teaching model explored earlier are equally relevant here. Teachers of all subjects, at all levels, could with benefit consider their children as apprentice writers in the subject, and use apprenticeship teaching strategies.

References and further reading

Austin, J and Howson, A (1979) Language and mathematics education, *Educational Studies in Mathematics*, 10, pp. 161–197.

Borasi, R and Rose, B (1989) Journal writing and mathematics instruction, *Educational Studies in Mathematics*, 20, pp. 347–365.

Brissenden, T (1988) *Talking about mathematics*. Oxford: Basil Blackwell.

Britton, J, Burgess, T, Martin, N, McLeod, A and Rosen, H (1975) *The development of writing abilities (11–18)*. Basingstoke: Macmillan.

Emig, J (1983) Writing as a mode of learning, in Goswami, D. and Butler, M. (eds) *The web of meaning: essays on writing, teaching and learning*, Upper Montclair, NJ: Boynton Cook, pp. 123–131.

Ervinck, G (1992) Mathematics as a foreign language, in *Proceedings of the 16th Conference of the International Group for the Psychology of Mathematics Education (Volume 3)*, Durham, NH: IGPME, pp. 217–233.

Gillman, L (1987) *Writing mathematics well: a manual for authors*. New York: The Mathematical Association of America.

Halliday, M (1974) Some aspects of sociolinguistics, in *Interactions between Linguistics and Mathematical Education Symposium*. Paris: UNESCO.

Kane, R (1968) The readability of mathematical English, *Journal of Research in Science Teaching*, 5, pp. 296–298.

Knuth, D, Larrabee, T and Roberts, P (1989) *Mathematical writing*. Washington, DC: The Mathematical Association of America.

Konior, J (1993) Research into the construction of mathematical texts, *Educational Studies in Mathematics*, 24, pp. 251–256.

Marks, G and Mousley, J (1990) Mathematics, education and genre: dare we make the process writing mistake again?, *Language and Education*, 4 (2), pp. 117–135. This is an important paper for two reasons. Firstly, it details one of the very few research studies into writing in mathematics in primary schools. Secondly, it applies the lessons gained from genre theory to the writing of mathematics – that is, unless teachers are alert to the problem, the tendency is simply to involve children only in recount writing in this subject, and to ignore the possibilities offered by other text types.

Martin, N, D'Arcy, P, Newton, B and Parker, R (1976) *Writing and learning across the curriculum 11–16*. London: Ward Lock.

Mathematical Association (1987) *Maths talk*. Cheltenham: Stanley Thornes.

Morgan, C (1998) *Writing mathematically: the discourse of investigation*. London: Falmer.

Rogers, A and MacDonald, C (1985) *Teaching writing for learning*. Edinburgh: Scottish Council for Research in Education.

Shuard, H and Rothery, A (1984) *Children reading mathematics*. London: Murray. This is the classic study of reading and mathematics. Although this book is dated now, the issues it raises, especially those to do with the readability of mathematics text-books, are still very relevant today.

Williams, Kenneth M (2003) Writing about the problem-solving process to improve problem-solving performance, *Mathematics Teacher*, 96 (3), pp. 185–187.

8 EXPLORING ELECTRONIC TEXTS ACROSS THE PRIMARY CURRICULUM

Chapter objectives:

The aim of this chapter is to introduce you to:
- *the ways in which electronic texts expand our ideas of literacy;*
- *the nature of electronic texts, which may be found in all areas of the curriculum;*
- *approaches to developing electronic literacy across the curriculum.*

Introduction: expanding literacy

I recently bought a new laptop computer and acquired an example of what has become known as a Tablet PC. This is different from normal laptops in two main ways: its screen can flip over onto the top of its keyboard, making it a little like a chunky A4 writing pad but with a surface of screen rather than paper; and it comes supplied with a special pen with which I can write on the screen, which then either treats my handwriting as a picture or converts it to computer text. As a machine, it is liberating. I can use it to handwrite notes in meetings, which are then automatically converted to typed text. I have a large collection of electronic books, any of which I can read easily on the tablet screen, so on long train or plane journeys it is like carrying 100 books with me to select my reading from.

One of the most exciting features of my new computer is that it came complete with a folder entitled 'My Magazines'. Inside this were electronic copies of a range of magazines (e.g. *Newsweek, Time, Personal Computer World, New Statesman*), all of which look very much like their printed versions, with a few crucial differences:

- **When I open one of these magazines, I get a double-page spread sideways on my A4 screen. This is at a good enough resolution for me to skim the page contents and, if I see an article or picture I want to look at in more detail, I touch it with the special pen and the view instantly zooms in so that I can read both text and pictures easily. Touch again and it zooms back out.**
- **If I find an article I am particularly interested in, I can select the whole of it with the pen and then copy it to a blank page. I can do this with several pieces, thus ending up with my own personal magazine of articles I really do want to read.**
- **I can use the pen to handwrite onto the magazine, making annotations easy. The touch of a button, however, makes these annotations disappear. (The touch of another button makes them return should I decide I erased them too quickly.)**
- **If I come across a technical word or phrase I am not too sure about, in most cases just hovering my pen above this makes a small window appear containing a definition.**
- **Hovering the pen over other words, phrases, pictures and captions brings up small windows containing lists of other places in the magazine that I can instantly jump to. For example, a piece about building a computer tells me that**

I need to include a graphics card. Holding my pen above the words 'graphics card' produces the suggestion that, if I want to read more about different kinds of graphic cards, I can go to another article in the magazine, and touching this text takes me to this article instantly. When I have finished reading about graphics cards I can instantly jump back to where I was originally.

Just a short period of experience with 'My Magazines' convinces me that I am engaged here in a completely new kind of reading. It is a reading in which I am in control of the order and sequence of text that I encounter, and in which I can actively contribute to creating the text I read. It is also a reading in which it is hard to relax, since I have to make decisions all the time.

Traditionally literacy has been simply defined as the condition of being able to read and write, and for most people this definition is adequate. However, it is becoming increasingly apparent that we need to expand our definition of literacy to include the reading and writing not only of printed texts but of electronic texts. Until recently, teachers could safely confine reading and writing activities to printed materials. Increasingly, however, reading and writing can be done electronically with the aid of a computer. Computers are being used to create and revise texts, to send and receive mail electronically, to present texts of all kinds on screen instead of in printed books, and to access large databases of texts. Electronic texts are becoming more prevalent as computers become an integral part of everyday experiences such as working, shopping, travelling and studying.

Clearly, teachers need to include electronic forms of reading and writing in the literacy experiences they offer their children. This creates two main issues for consideration, both of which I will explore in this chapter:

- **How are electronic texts different from printed texts?**
- **How can learners be prepared to read and write electronically?**

The characteristics of electronic texts

In this section, I will briefly discuss four fundamental differences between printed and electronic texts, namely, that:

- **readers and texts can interact;**
- **reading can be guided;**
- **electronic texts have different structures;**
- **electronic texts employ new symbols.**

I will try here to go beyond the merely surface differences between the two media. A screen looks different from a page but that in itself need not imply a different way of reading the text in this medium. There are many electronic texts which are simply print texts put onto a screen, and these do not challenge readers any more than print texts. Increasingly, however, electronic texts are being created which do more than duplicate print, and it is on the characteristics of these more adventurous texts that I will focus here.

Readers and texts can interact

Reading is often described as an interaction between a reader and a text. However, readers and printed texts cannot literally interact. A printed text cannot respond to a reader, nor do printed texts invite modification by a reader. To describe reading as an interaction simply reflects the fact that the outcomes of reading are the result of factors associated with the text and factors associated with the reader.

Because reading is interactive in this sense, a successful reader must be mentally active during reading. Readers clearly vary in their cognitive capabilities and because of this a basic part of understanding the process of reading has come to be seen as understanding the reader. Features of printed texts, such as the use of illustrations, have not been entirely ignored, but it is true to say that the role of the printed text in the reading process has not generally been emphasised in discussion about the reading process. One reason for this greater interest in readers than in texts is that texts are static and inert once they are printed. When a writer's intended meaning is viewed as frozen in a printed form, it is only logical to focus on a reader's efforts to construct meaning from this print.

Successful readers of printed texts know that it is their responsibility to derive meaning from those texts, and they approach the task of reading accordingly. A printed text cannot clarify itself if the reader is having difficulty understanding it. Readers may consciously interact with a text by applying their own knowledge to it, but they cannot literally carry on a dialogue with a printed text.

Electronic texts, on the other hand, can involve a literal interaction between texts and readers (Daniel and Reinking, 1987). Using the capabilities of the computer, reading electronic texts can become a dialogue. Electronic texts can be programmed to adapt to an individual reader's needs and interests during reading, which may in turn affect the strategies readers use to read and comprehend texts.

Research insight

Electronic interactive texts

Reinking and Rickman (1990) explored the use of electronic texts which provided readers, on request, with definitions of difficult words as they were reading. The effects of reading such texts were compared with the reading of printed texts accompanied by conventional resources such as dictionaries and glossaries. It was found that 9- to 13-year-olds reading the interactive computer texts investigated more word meanings, remembered the meanings of more words, and understood more of the experimental text.

Other research (e.g. Reinking and Schreiner, 1985) has suggested that readers' comprehension of texts increases when they read electronic texts providing a variety of support options, such as definitions of difficult words, illustrations (sometimes animated) of processes described, or maps of a text's structure.

In the future it will be possible to design electronic texts so that they respond to certain characteristics of the reader. Imagine a screen-based text that changes its format, content and speed of presentation depending on the rate at which a reader reads it. Possible already are texts which, at the end of each screen, ask the reader to choose what next to read. Interactive texts like these offer many potential texts. It would be possible to read them several times without reading exactly the same text twice.

Reading can be guided

The previous examples illustrate how electronic texts can respond to individual readers. This capability makes reading literally an interactive experience in which texts play an active role during reading. But not only can a computer present texts that respond to a reader, it can determine which portion of a text a reader is permitted to see. Thus, electronic texts introduce the capability of influencing what a reader attends to during reading.

One example of how this feature might be used is the information text presented to readers one screen at a time. At the end of their reading of one screen, the readers are forced to respond to a question designed to judge their understanding of what they have read so far. Depending on their answers to these questions, the computer selects the next screen of text for them to read, thus allowing the possibility of reviewing misunderstood material, or building upon existing understandings. Electronic text therefore can become a deliberate teaching tool.

Electronic texts have different structures

The idea that textual information might be structured differently if it is stored electronically is not new. In 1945, Vannevar Bush, a US presidential adviser, proposed that researchers develop electronic means for linking related information in a large database of microfilm documents. In 1960, Ted Nelson introduced the term *hypertext* in referring to electronic documents structured as non-linear, non-sequential texts (see Lunin and Rada, 1989). Hypertexts have three attributes that separate them from conventionally structured printed texts.

- **A database consisting of distinct units of text (which may consist of words, pictures, sounds or moving images).**
- **A network connecting the textual units (the textual units are referred to as 'nodes' in the network).**
- **Electronic tools for moving flexibly through the network.**

The technology available when the concept of hypertext was first proposed did not allow easy and widespread implementation of the idea but rapid developments in computing power over the past few years have made hypertexts not only possible but, through the medium of the internet and world wide web, virtually inescapable. Web pages are coded in **H**yper**T**ext **M**arkup **L**anguage – HTML.

Practical task

Examining an HTML page

The internet address www.warwick.ac.uk/staff/D.J.Wray *will take you to an example of a simple web page on which some features of hypertext have been implemented. This page contains a mixture of textual and graphic elements and is designed as the central node of a network of connecting texts.*

Explore the page to see if you can find examples of the following hypertext features. In each case, what is the function of this feature within the web page?

Feature	What is the function of this?
Hot spot	
Link to other web pages	
Email link	
Form posting link	
Navigation bar	

An example of a much more complex web page can be found at **www.bbc.co.uk**. Here virtually every element on the page will, if clicked with the mouse, lead to a different page and some of these will produce sound and/or moving images.

The fact that electronic texts can be structured so differently to print texts brings the difficulties inherent in electronic literacy into sharp focus. Becoming literate for electronic reading will require that readers become familiar with the nonlinear, non-sequential text structures that are the natural form of electronic texts. They will also need to develop appropriate strategies for reading such texts. Reading web pages like the BBC home page is not straightforward and many otherwise skilful readers readily admit to getting lost quite easily within such material.

Electronic texts employ new symbols

Part of being literate is being good at using all the symbols that are available for communicating meaning in a written language. Readers and writers must know the conventions for using these symbols and understand how they convey meaning in a written language. Such awareness includes being able to use and interpret symbols beyond words themselves, such as graphic aids (e.g. illustrations and tables), organisational units (e.g. chapters), and typographical markers (e.g. underlining or italics).

Electronic texts incorporate more and different symbols than those used in printed texts. For example, symbols used with electronic texts but not with printed texts include: flashing, animated or moving visual displays; sound effects; and video. These elements create new possibilities for communicating meaning and they give rise to the need for new conventions for using them in conjunction with traditional print.

The availability of more symbols is problematic in the development of electronic literacy, partly because agreed conventions for using the various symbols have not yet been established. Part of the problem is that the symbols available for use in electronic texts continue to expand rapidly, and the conventions for using them change with each advance in computer technology. To take a few examples, most literate people today will be familiar with the meanings of many of the symbols included in the screenshot in Figure 8.1.

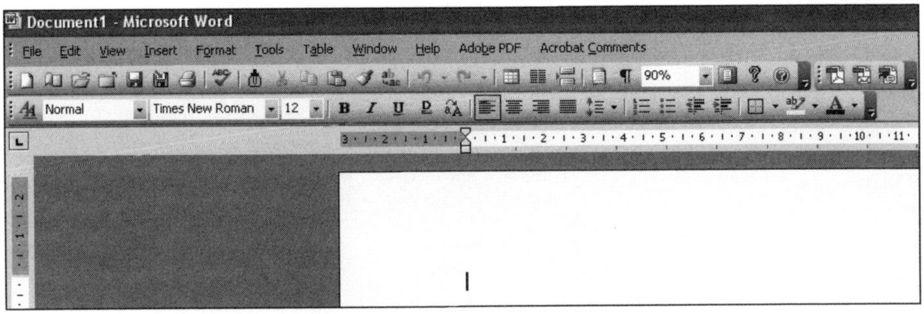

Figure 8.1 *Text control symbols*

There may be some problematic symbols even here, in perhaps the most widely used computer writing environment in the world. This is especially true because the interface permits customisation, so what we have here is the Microsoft Word template which I myself use. Not every Word user will have defined the 'gluepot' symbol (ninth symbol from the left on the top row of icons) to mean 'Select the whole document' – but it works for me!

Other sets of symbols may be more difficult. Figure 8.2 (see page 112), for example, shows a combination which will be very familiar to anyone who uses the web as a source of information, yet its use is not easy.

We know this is a PDF file (but possibly not what those initials stand for – portable document format), and we know that we need at least Acrobat Reader on our computers to read these files, but many people are not at all clear about how to navigate around such documents. Just what is the function of that little hand on the left of the toolbar? And why does that button with the binocular picture not immediately bring our view of the document closer? In fact, there are a number of ways to zoom in and out of the document using the selection of icons to the right of the tiny magnifying glass with the plus sign. These difficulties increase when you try to open the document on a different computer, because the software may have been set up differently and a quite different set of symbols used.

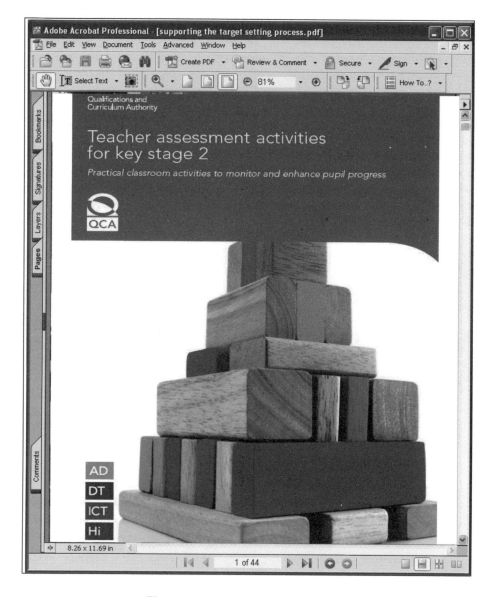

Figure 8.2 *Document control symbols*

An example of how electronic texts may change the relations between symbols is that in electronic texts, graphic material is more closely integrated with prose. In printed materials, prose and graphic elements such as tables, charts and diagrams are more likely to be seen as separate symbol systems, each with its own symbols and conventions for using them. In electronic texts, however, prose, sounds and graphics may merge together. Think of a web page which, when opened, has text appearing at its foot and gradually scrolling up and eventually into the distance, rather like the opening sequence of the film *Star Wars*. Only this is not in a galaxy far, far away: this is here, today and is typical of the extra demands reading electronic texts can make upon the reader.

Practical task

Exploring electronic text symbols

Have a look at some other computer working environments in which icons are used. Simple examples might be Paint (on Windows XP computers this is usually found by clicking the 'Start' button, then selecting 'All Programs' then 'Accessories') or Notepad (same procedure as for Paint). Both of these programs use text-based (rather than icon-based) menus, so they might be thought of as simpler environments. But each carries its own difficulties. In Paint, for example, what menu combination would you use to crop a picture (slice off an unwanted portion of it)? (Hint: There are two ways of doing this – both irreversible, so be careful to save an image before trying.)

Now look at the environment for the program Windows Media Player. This has extra complications because you can actually use several different environments in this program. Try clicking Control + 2 and look at the difference in the icons used to control the program. Click Control + 1 to get back to the original look.

You should be able to see how using such programs demands knowledge of some quite sophisticated symbol systems – new literacies. And these are in fact quite simple programs.

Developing electronic literacy

The increasing use of electronic texts makes it clear that teachers need to begin to think seriously about how activities aimed at developing electronic literacy can be built into normal classroom literacy teaching. Ideally, these activities should meet three criteria.

1. They should help develop children's print-based literacy as well as their electronic literacy. Although electronic literacy is likely to become more and more important, it is unlikely in the foreseeable future that it will cause the demise of traditional literacy.

2. They should involve authentic communication tasks for children. Enough is known about the motivational and learning benefits of children seeing for themselves the purposes of reading and writing for us to be fairly confident that authenticity is a powerful benchmark of effectiveness in literacy work. Activities which feature electronic reading and writing have a head start in authenticity since most children will perceive these media as important in the world outside school.

3. They should engage children in critical thinking about the nature of printed and electronic texts as well as about the topics they contain. As we have seen, there are some fundamental differences between these media and children need to develop critical awareness of these, including when one is more appropriate than another, the effects of each upon the reader and the process of authorship appropriate to each.

There are a number of uses of electronic literacy in the classroom.

Electronic books

Some of the earliest reading materials available on the computer were adaptations of existing print texts. The American companies Discis (*Thomas' Snowsuit, The Paperbag Princess*) and Broderbund (*Arthur's Teacher Troubles, Just Grandma and Me*) were the first to have any major impact. These were simply collections of books which had been converted to work from CD-ROM. Of course, they were not just placed on a CD, but were enhanced to harness the power of the computer. Each CD contained a multimedia book which would read itself to a child while sound effects and music complemented the story. The books presented many options, such as varying speeds of reading, explanations of words, and even options to have the book read in a different language. The idea was that, as a child's reading ability grew, he/she could use the computer just to say the words he/she could not read.

Later, British companies such as Sherston Software began to produce much smaller talking books, each title being compressed to fit on a single floppy disk. The simplicity of the Sherston system meant that these books had a major impact in UK schools, especially when the best-selling British reading scheme, Oxford Reading Tree, adopted the system to produce electronic versions of its books.

Most electronic books produced for school use have similar facilities. They all provide on-screen text, illustrated with pictures. By clicking on certain icons, the text can be read aloud by the computer, or the pictures can be animated. They all also provide the facility for the reader to click on individual words (phrases in the case of the American books) to hear these read aloud.

Research insight

Research into the use of electronic books

A number of research studies have investigated the impact of electronic books on children's reading. Medwell (1996, 1998), for example, explored whether talking books could help young children learn to read traditional print texts and, if so, how they supported children's reading. In Medwell's studies, Reception/Year 1 children used the Sherston Naughty Stories and the Oxford Reading Tree Talking Stories. The results of these two studies suggested that talking books do help young children to learn to read traditional texts and particularly helped children to understand the meanings of the stories. Medwell found that children who used the electronic versions of the books learned more than children who only used print versions, but that the most learning was achieved by children who read the print versions with their teachers and then used the electronic versions by themselves. This suggests that, although electronic books can help children progress in reading, they complement rather than replace the role of the skilled teacher of reading.

Research, therefore, seems to suggest that electronic books can help children develop as readers, but that they need to be used circumspectly by teachers if the maximum impact is to be obtained.

Finding out with the computer

In many ways, information text was made for computerised presentation. Most readers do not read information books in the linear way they may approach fiction text and adopt instead a pseudo-hypertextual approach, focused around the core node of the contents or index page, from which links are made to other text units. Having such text on a computer simply makes such an approach more efficient. Rather than having to physically turn the pages of a book, the reader can just click on a link to move to the relevant information.

One of the unfortunate by-products of this is that the already significant tendency of children to copy from information books is likely to be worsened by the use of electronic information text. After all, selecting, copying and pasting material from a CD-ROM or the internet is a lot easier than having to write out material from a book. There are a number of tried-and-tested strategies for helping children avoid straight copying when they use information books, and I have discussed the use of some of these earlier in this book. They work just as well with computer-based material.

A systematic treatment of ways to avoid children copying information text can be found in Wray and Lewis (1997). They recommend thinking about information finding as a series of mental processes, an analysis they refer to as the EXIT (EXtending Interactions with Texts) model (see Table 8.1).

Crucial to avoiding copying is the thinking that children are encouraged to do before they begin to use information sources. Wray and Lewis recommend getting children to consider what they already know about a topic before formulating some questions to which they would like to find answers. This then lessens the possibility of them approaching information sources looking to record everything they find. A particularly useful strategy here is to ask children to use grids such as the KWL (See Figure 3.3 in Chapter 3) to record the process of their information research.

Wray and Lewis also suggest that, when children are reading information text, they read actively. One strategy for active reading is for readers to mark text which they think is significant. In printed text this can involve the use of highlighter pens and there is usually an equivalent to this for screen-based text. In Microsoft Word this involves clicking the 'Text Highlight' button, selecting a highlight colour and then using the mouse to select appropriate text. More than one colour can be used in the same document, thus allowing information relevant to a number of questions to be picked out.

Another active reading strategy is for children to restructure the information they read into one of a variety of other forms. Children might go to information sources armed with a pre-drawn grid which will both guide them in their information search and help them structure the information they find for subsequent reporting. With electronic text, this would be a word-processed grid which they keep open in a window on the screen, while they browse information sources in another window. Noting information on the grid can then be done using the keyboard and the results printed out and shared.

Process stages	Questions
1. Activation of previous knowledge	1. What do I already know about this subject?
2. Establishing purposes	2. What do I need to find out and what will I do with the information?
3. Locating information	3. Where and how will I get this information?
4. Adopting an appropriate strategy	4. How should I use this source of information to get what I need?
5. Interacting with text	5. What can I do to help me understand this better?
6. Monitoring understanding	6. What can I do if there are parts I don't understand?
7. Making a record	7. What should I make a note of from this information?
8. Evaluating information	8. Which items of information should I believe and which should I keep an open mind about?
9. Assisting memory	9. How can I help myself remember the important parts?
10. Communicating information	10. How should I let other people know about this?

Figure 8.3 *The EXIT model: stages and questions*

Problem-solving with texts

There are a range of textual problem-solving activities (generically referred to as DARTs – directed activities relating to texts) which have been shown to be useful ways of encouraging children to interact purposefully with printed texts. Activities in this range include cloze, where children have to work together to suggest possible words to fill deletions in a text; and sequencing, where a group of children have to work out a meaningful order for a text which has been cut into sections and mixed up. What these activities have in common is that they involve group discussion of disrupted texts and their main aim is to recreate meaningful text.

An early attempt to adapt activities like this to electronic text was the computer program known as Developing TRAY. This program was written initially for use with secondary slow-reading children. The name derives from the idea of a print gradually coming into focus in a photographer's developing tray. Starting with a screen showing only punctuation and a series of dashes to represent letters, the children gradually reconstruct the extract, initially by 'buying' letters then by predicting words or phrases as the text becomes clearer. A number of research studies, both at secondary (e.g. Johnson, 1985) and primary (Haywood and Wray, 1988) levels, have suggested that experience with the program involves the use of high-level problem-solving skills, analysis of data, decision-making about strategies, the creation and interpretation of meaning and hypothesis forming and testing.

TRAY is now 20 years old, which for educational software is old indeed, but the fact that a modernised version is still available is testimony to its abiding usefulness in developing children's reading. It is usually found now as part of text problem-solving suites of programs (often given names such as 'word detectives') which include computer versions of other DARTs.

A more recent addition to teachers' technological armouries is the interactive whiteboard, which has a great deal of potential in the teaching of reading. The whiteboard allows the information appearing on a computer screen to be projected onto a much larger surface but when it is there it can be interacted with – text can be added with a pen, moved, annotated or deleted. This means that the interactivity which is characteristic of electronic text can now be carried out as a shared activity with large groups of children. A simple example of this is the sequencing activity briefly mentioned earlier. Normally this is done with sections of printed text which have physically been cut up, and children move the sections around, experimenting with possible orders until they find one they can agree on. Because of the size of the text and the need to handle the sections, it is normal for this activity to involve three or four children at most. With an interactive whiteboard, however, the sections of text appear in large type on the board and each can be moved around using the board pen. This makes whole-class discussion of such a text possible.

Using word processors

Many teachers have been impressed by the way even quite young children quickly learn how to use word-processing programs on the computer, and seem to be able to improve the quality of their writing by doing so. What is it about word processors that leads to this improvement?

To answer this question we need firstly to look at the ways in which our understanding of the process of writing has changed over the last few years. Perhaps the most significant feature of this change has been the realisation that to expect children to produce well thought-out, interesting writing, correctly spelt and punctuated, grammatical and neatly written, at one sitting, is to expect the impossible. Even experienced adult writers do not work that way, and will confirm that any writing other than the most trivial goes through several drafts before it is considered finished. Many teachers encourage their children to approach writing in this way – that is, to write drafts which can then be revised, shared with other readers, discussed, and edited before reaching their final versions. At Key Stage 2, the National

Curriculum requires that children be given opportunities to do this, and spells out the process in some detail:

Children should be taught to:
- *plan – note and develop initial ideas;*
- *draft – develop ideas from the plan into structured written text;*
- *revise – alter and improve the draft;*
- *proofread – check the draft for spelling and punctuation errors, omissions or repetitions;*
- *present – prepare a neat, correct and clear final copy.*

The use of the word processor as a writing tool reinforces this drafting process. Writing on a computer screen does not have the permanence of writing on paper. Everything about it becomes provisional, and can be altered at the touch of a key. This provisional nature of word-processed writing has very important implications for the way children think about and set about their writing.

A significant reason why children may find it difficult to accept the idea of writing as provisional when it is done on paper is the fact that, if they wish to change their writing, this will usually involve rewriting it. The sheer physical effort of this will persuade some children to adopt a much more studied, once-and-for-all approach to their writing. With a word processor, however, alterations can be made on the screen and there is no need to rewrite. This facility for immediate error correction allows children to approach writing much more experimentally. They soon become prepared to try things out and alter them several times if need be. They also begin to be able to live with uncertainty. If, for example, they are unsure of particular spellings, they can try an approximation and check it later, without breaking the flow of their writing ideas. 'We'll do the spellings afterwards' becomes a familiar strategy.

Another significant feature provided by word processing is the facility to cut and paste text electronically. Sections of text can easily be moved around the piece of writing. This allows writers to re-sequence their writing with little effort and to experiment with different sequences. It is, of course, possible to achieve this with pencil and paper by using arrows, or with scissors and glue, but neither of these methods compares with the simplicity of the word processor. Again this facility increases the provisionality of writing. Not only can text be changed at will, it can also be rearranged in any number of ways.

Most word processors have the facility to search through texts for particular words or markers, and then replace them with other words. This can assist children's writing in a variety of ways. Firstly, it allows them to change their minds easily. If, for example, they have written a story about a boy called Pete and suddenly decide they really want it to be about a girl called Mary, these details can be altered throughout the text by a couple of key presses.

Secondly, it provides a way of dealing easily with consistent misspellings. If, for example, a child regularly spells *occasion* as *ocassion*, or *should* as *sholud*, he can be asked to check these words after finishing his writing. Having ascertained the correct spelling, he can then use the word processor to alter every occurrence of the misspelling at one go. Most word processors allow the user to decide whether each individual occurrence should be altered. Usually the user has to press 'Y' or 'N' as appropriate. This can be useful if there are words the child regularly confuses, such as *there* and *their*, or *hear* and *here*. Being asked to consider each one in turn encourages children to become more aware of the contexts in which each one is appropriate.

A further use of the search and replace facility is to eliminate some of the distraction caused when children search for the spellings of words they are unsure of. These can be entered at first using a marker (say, the initial letter plus ***). When the first draft is done, the children can then find the correct spellings and use the replace facility to change their markers. This is an extremely useful technique in writing, and once children understand it they can use it to save themselves a great deal of writing effort. Frequently used words can also be entered as markers, and typed once in full at the end of the writing. This was actually how I wrote the words *word processor* in the present chapter.

A further important feature of word processing has already been hinted at. If a piece of writing can be saved to disk, it can then be re-read and re-edited at a later date. The facility to edit previously created text has a very important effect. Writing ceases to be a one-shot exercise, with everything having to be done correctly at one sitting. There is, in fact, no limit to the number of times the writer can return to it, and make changes as easily as the first time. This adds to writing the important dimension of time. Ideas can be considered over time, new ideas can be taken on board, and writing can be discussed with others. This has the effect of making writing a much more thoughtful process.

Allowing children the time for the reflective editing implied by this may seem to involve the dedication of large amounts of computer time to very few children. This, however, need not be so because of the facility to print out the writing that children produce. They can then take away this printout, and work on revising it away from the computer. This can involve crossing sections out, scribbling extra ideas in, and discussing the draft with anyone they wish. They can then return to the computer when it is again free, to call up their draft and make any changes to it they feel necessary, before printing again, whereupon this process can be repeated.

Using hard copy for initial revision has an extra advantage in addition to its freeing of computer time for others to use. By altering printed text and especially by crossing out, children can begin to lose their fear of making writing messy. Because of their earlier educational experience, many children approach writing under what has been termed 'the tyranny of the flawless page'. They are extremely reluctant to do anything to disturb this flawlessness. A printout, however, has cost them little physical effort and can always be repeated if need be. It need not, therefore, be kept flawless. This change in children's attitudes towards writing has great significance for their future approach to it, and helps convince them of the provisional nature of writing.

There is, of course, little point in using a word processor with children unless their work can be printed out. Printouts are available, however, in not one but multiple copies, which can be of immense benefit. It is a simple matter to take sufficient copies of a piece of writing for the child to have one to go in a folder, the teacher to have one to display, one to be placed in the child's record portfolio, and one to be taken home to parents. The significance of this is readily seen by considering what happens with non-word-processed writing which a teacher wishes to put on display. Often this results in the child having to copy it out, with consequent negative effects on that child's motivation to write.

A further advantage of printed writing is its levelling effect. Many children have poor images of themselves as writers not because they lack ability in the composing aspects of the process, but simply because they find handwriting a strain. In word processing, poor handwriting is no longer a problem. Children with poor physical co-ordination can write as well as those with good, and the sense of achievement these children get can be enormous. This is not to argue, of course, that clear, efficient handwriting is no longer necessary. Children will still need to be taught handwriting. It does mean, though, that lack of ability in this aspect of writing need not assume the overarching, debilitating effects it often does. It also means that teachers can get beyond the presentation aspects of children's writing when attempting to make judgements about their abilities. Most children will need help of some kind with their writing, but it is easy for teachers to concentrate this help on the physical aspect simply because this is what stands out immediately. If this aspect can be discounted then teachers can direct their help to other, more important parts of the writing process.

Children's word-processed text can be rearranged in various ways on the computer. This makes it possible for their writing to emerge looking very much like that in 'real' books, with consequent benefits for their motivation to write. The aspect of this which is usually discovered first is justification.

The effects of this can be seen in the following example of the writing of 9-year-old Jennifer, who has been finding out about rabbits. Her account first looked like this:

Before I began this topic I thought that the male rabbits were the ones who dug the warrens. But when I read about it, I found out that it was actual the females who did all the work, as usual!
I also learnt that the passages or burrows are up to 3m long and 15cm wide so the rabbits can get through easily.
Secondly I learnt that the warren can be over 30 years old and around 30 rabbits can live in one.
Finally I learnt that the rabbits warren has lots of ways in and out, so if one is blocked a rabbit can get in another.

Figure 8.4

This was then corrected, justified and the font altered to produce this:

Before I began this topic I thought that the male rabbits were the ones who dug the warrens. But when I read about it, I found out that it was actually the females who did all the work, as usual!
I also learnt that the passages or burrows are up to 3m long and 15cm wide so the rabbits can get through easily.
Secondly I learnt that the warren can be over 30 years old and around 30 rabbits can live in one.
Finally I learnt that the rabbits' warren has lots of ways in and out, so if one is blocked a rabbit can get in another.

Figure 8.5

Jennifer was delighted with the look of this and commented that it was just like in an information book.

This ability to rearrange text can be taken further by altering the format of the text. If the writing had been done for a class newspaper, it could be formatted with narrower columns.

Before I began this topic I thought that the male rabbits were the ones who dug the warrens. But when I read about it, I found out that it was actually the females who did all the work, as usual!
I also learnt that the passages or burrows are up to 3m long and 15cm wide so the rabbits can get through easily.

Secondly I learnt that the warren can be over 30 years old and around 30 rabbits can live in one.
Finally I learnt that the rabbits' warren has lots of ways in and out, so if one is blocked a rabbit can get in another

Figure 8.6

Most word processors also permit writing to be produced in a variety of type styles, or fonts, from Script to Gothic. So the above writing might be produced as:

Before I began this topic I thought that the male rabbits were the ones who dug the warrens. But when I read about it, I found out that it was actually the females who did all the work, as usual!
I also learnt that the passages or burrows are up to 3m long and 15cm wide so the rabbits can get through easily.
Secondly I learnt that the warren can be over 30 years old and around 30 rabbits can live in one.
Finally I learnt that the rabbits' warren has lots of ways in and out, so if one is blocked a rabbit can get in another.

Figure 8.7

Or:

Before I began this topic I thought that the male rabbits were the ones who dug the warrens. But when I read about it, I found out that it was actually the females who did all the work, as usual! I also learnt that the **passages** or burrows are up to 3m long and 15cm wide so the rabbits can get through easily.
Secondly I learnt that the **warren** can be over 30 years old and around 30 rabbits can live in one. Finally I learnt that the **rabbits'** warren has lots of ways in and out, so if one is blocked a rabbit can get in another.

Figure 8.8

Such features can enhance children's writing a great deal, and have the effect of making children enjoy writing more. They also give rise to a great deal of discussion about the appropriateness of each feature, which can develop children's awareness of text. Is a script font really appropriate for an information text, for example?

Word processors can be used as writing tools for individual children. This is, however, an uneconomic use of expensive equipment and it does not make best use of their particular features. Because writing appears on what looks like a television screen, it is much more public than the usual pencil-and-paper process. It positively invites sharing. A more usual way of using the word processor is for children to write in collaboration with one or two of their classmates. This enables discussion and debate to take place about the writing, which has an almost inevitable beneficial effect upon the quality of what is produced.

Improved quality in writing is the chief reason for the use of word processors with children. There are several reasons why this happens, one of which – the opportunity for discussion and debate – has already been referred to. There is also the distancing effect word processors seem to have. They allow children to stand back from their writing and read it with fresh eyes. This distancing permits them to make changes they would perhaps otherwise not realise were necessary.

There are, therefore, several excellent reasons why word processors should feature prominently in the writing experience of primary children.

Practical task

Shared writing with a word processor

A word processor can be used as a medium for shared writing, although, of course, the presentation device used will need to be sufficiently large for the writing on it to be read easily by the whole class. This requires either a very large computer screen (a 21" screen may just be large enough), a data projector to project the computer image onto a large screen or wall, or an electronic whiteboard.

Here are a few examples of possible shared writing lessons that that you might adapt and try out with children.

1. Word level work – Year 4

Objective: To spell regular verb endings –s, –ed, –ing

Set the word processor to display a large font, e.g. 28 point, and type in the following list of words: care, come, face, file, give, glue, hope, ice, joke, like, live, love, make. *Type* ing *after the first few, using a different font. Explain the rule about dropping the final e, and delete the spaces between the word and the suffix. Finally delete the e as well, giving a dynamic demonstration of how the joining of stem and suffix and the deletion of the final e are part of the same action. Do this with a couple of examples.*

Give ... ing	give ing	giveing	giving
Hope ... ing	hope ing	hopeing	hoping

Now let individual children come to the computer to carry out the same action. If you have a talking word processor, you can listen to the sounds of the words and then compare them to some common spelling mistakes such as comming *and* hopping.

2. Sentence level work – Year 4

Objective: to identify common adverbs with an –ly suffix

Set the word processor to display a large font, e.g. 28 point, and type in the following list of –ly adverbs: quickly, slowly, swiftly, sluggishly, rapidly, unhurriedly. *Highlight the ly and then increase the size (on most word processors this can be done by holding down Ctrl + Shift and > (greater than)).*

quickly   quick**ly**   quick**ly**   quick**ly**

Let some children try this with other words. Such animations are a good way of fixing certain letter strings in children's minds.

3. Sentence level work – Year 3

Objective: To recognise the function of verbs in sentences, and to use verb tenses in writing

Use a large font size and write some simple sentences without their verbs, e.g. Alexander all the chocolate bars.

Ask the children: what is missing? Where should the missing word go? What possibilities are there for this missing word or phrase? Type one suggestion into the sentence, using a font which stands out. Use copy and paste to reproduce the same sentence five or so times. In each sentence, use a different verb, or a variation on the same verb.

Alexander **ate** all the chocolate bars.

Alexander **grabbed** all the chocolate bars.

Alexander **hated** all the chocolate bars.

Alexander **will eat** all the chocolate bars.

Alexander **eats** all the chocolate bars.

Alexander **has eaten** all the chocolate bars.

Discuss all the different meanings that this creates. Children should now be in a position to write their own versions of this changing sentence.

As an extension to this activity, you could try adding adverbs (Year 4 – identify adverbs and … notice where they occur in sentences and how they are used to qualify the meanings of verbs). Does a different position affect the meaning of the sentence?

Alexander **quickly** ate all the chocolate bars.

Quickly, Alexander ate all the chocolate bars.

Alexander ate all the chocolate bars **quickly**.

4. Sentence level work – Year 5

Objective: To investigate clauses through understanding how clauses are connected

Have on the screen/whiteboard some examples of jumbled sentences, that is, sentences in which the main and subordinate clauses do not match.

Walking slowly along the road, Libby finally forced herself out of bed.

When Mum shouted upstairs, James suddenly heard the hoot of a car behind him.

Discuss these sentences and demonstrate how, by using 'drag and drop' or 'cut and paste', they can be sorted out.

Try moving the subordinate clause to a different position in the sentence, and discuss any changes to the meaning that this causes.

Walking slowly along the road, James suddenly heard the hoot of a car behind him.

James suddenly heard the hoot of a car behind him, **walking slowly along the road.**

Children can then be asked to construct their complex sentences using this pattern, and experiment with different clause positioning.

Summary

In this chapter I have explored some of the ways in which text is changing with the advent of new technologies. Central to my argument here is that as text changes, so the process of reading and writing changes to match this. Reading and writing electronic texts is not the same as reading and writing printed texts, which means that teaching children to read and write needs to develop too. In the final section of the chapter, I briefly examined some teaching approaches involving electronic texts. Inevitably, however, teaching lags behind the world outside and it is certain that we have only just begun to respond in schools to the changing nature of text. There are exciting changes still to come.

References and further reading

Daniel, DB and Reinking, D (1987) The construct of legibility in electronic reading environments, in Reinking, D. (ed.) *Reading and computers: Issues for theory and practice* (pp. 24–39). New York: Teachers College Press.

Haywood, S and Wray, D (1988) Using TRAY, a text reconstruction program, with top infants, *Educational Review*, 40 (1).

Johnson, V (1985) Introducing the microcomputer into English: An evaluation of TRAY as a program using problem-solving as a strategy for developing reading skills, *British Journal of Educational Technology*, 16 (3), pp. 208–218.

Lunin, LR and Rada, R (1989) Hypertext: Introduction and overview, *Journal of the American Society for Information Science*, 40, pp. 159–163.

Medwell, J (1996) Talking books and reading, *Reading*, 30 (1), pp. 41–46.

Medwell, J (1998) The talking books project: some further insights into the use of talking books to develop reading, *Reading*, 32 (1), pp. 3–9.

Reinking, D and Rickman, SS (1990) The effects of computer-mediated texts on the vocabulary learning and comprehension of intermediate-grade readers, *Journal of Reading Behavior*, 22, pp. 395–411.

Reinking, D and Schreiner, R (1985) The effects of computer-mediated text on measures of reading comprehension and reading behavior, *Reading Research Quarterly*, 20, pp. 536–552.

Wray, D and Lewis, M (1997) *Extending literacy*. London: Routledge. Perhaps the best source of information about the new literacies made available by new technology, especially the internet, is the website run by the New Literacies Research Team at the University of Connecticut: **www.newliteracies.uconn. edu/**. This team is led by Don Leu, who is the world leader currently in thinking about the ways in which new technologies affect literacy. Many of his articles can be read at his personal website: **www.sp.uconn.edu/~djleu/**.

INDEX